THE
HUNGRY
STUDENT
VEGAN
COOKBOOK

**MORE THAN 200 DELICIOUS AND
NUTRITIOUS VEGAN RECIPES**

hamlyn

SOY TOFU SALAD WITH CORIANDER

MUSHROOM STROGANOFF

An Hachette UK Company
www.hachette.co.uk

First published in Great Britain in 2018 by Spruce,
an imprint of Octopus Publishing Group Ltd,
Carmelite House, 50 Victoria Embankment
London EC4Y 0DZ
www.octopusbooks.co.uk

This edition published in 2022 by Hamlyn

ISBN 978-0-60063-749-3

A CIP catalogue record for this book is available
from the British Library

Printed and bound in China

10 9 8 7 6 5 4 3 2 1

Standard level spoon measurement are used
in all recipes.
1 tablespoon = one 15 ml spoon
1 teaspoon = one 5 ml spoon

Both imperial and metric measurements have been
given in all recipes. Use one set of measurements only
and not a mixture of both.

Ovens should be preheated to the specific temperature
– if using a fan-assisted oven, follow manufacturer's
instructions for adjusting the time and the temperature.

Pepper should be freshly ground black pepper unless
otherwise stated.

Check the label on all ingredients to ensure they are
suitable for vegans.

FSC
www.fsc.org

MIX
Paper from
responsible sources
FSC® C008047

RAW CHERRY & ALMOND CAKE
WITH CHOCOLATE GANACHE

CONTENTS

INTRODUCTION

Moving away from home is both an exciting and an uncertain time. You're about to embark on the next stage of your life—and the first one that involves fending for yourself. From working out how to operate complex appliances, such as the washing machine, to setting your own alarm clock, doing your own grocery shopping, and giving up the luxury of the mom and dad taxi service, going to college is a steep learning curve—and that's before you've even started the learning part!

For the first few days or weeks, food is probably not the highest entry on your list of priorities—you eat when you're hungry, and as long as it's palatable and fills you, it's fine. But there will come a point when you crave a meal that doesn't involve putting a random ingredient between two slices of bread, or scraping the contents of a can into a bowl and watching it turn sadly inside a microwave. And that's when you'll unpack this book from the box under your bed and flick through to find the makings of a decent dinner.

Fortunately, you don't need to be an accomplished chef to prepare any of the recipes in the following pages. You presumably have a certain amount of common sense and intelligence or you wouldn't be going to college—and that's pretty much all you'll need to prepare, cook, and bake yourself to foodie heaven. As a vegan student, you've no doubt come across all the stereotypes imaginable, but there's absolutely no reason why you can't eat well and healthily while sticking to a budget. With a little forward planning, a few key utensils, and a well-stocked refrigerator and pantry, you can enjoy homemade meals every day, with plenty of delicious snacks and treats thrown in for good measure.

PLANNING AND BUDGETING

Before you arrive in your new digs, it's a good idea to have a conversation with your housemates about how the grocery shopping and cooking is going to work. Will you be shopping together as a household or each buy your own food? Will you be taking turns cooking or just decide on the day and cook for whoever is at home?

Food that disappears from the refrigerator and people who owe money for shopping are issues that can quickly escalate into major disputes. Not everyone has the same ideas about communal shopping and cooking and, while most people are happy to pull their weight and contribute time, money, and some effort into stocking the cupboards, preparing meals, and cleaning up afterward, it's not a given. If everyone agrees to a few basic house rules in the first days, there's less chance of people falling out when someone drinks the soy milk by mistake, or if after a night out late someone helps themselves to the ingredients you've bought for a special dinner.

If you will be buying groceries as a household, online shopping may a good idea, because it means that you don't all have to physically go to the supermarket on a weekly basis—you can shop from your accomodations and take your time to work out the best deals and the most convenient delivery time. Order all your basics together so the bill can be split evenly. The same applies when it comes to cooking; choose some easy midweek meals and share the cooking. But when it comes to ordering speciality ingredients, or an item that only one person wants, it's best to do this separately.

BUDGETING CHECKLIST:

- Make a weekly meal plan. This won't be set in stone, because plans change and not everyone will be at home every night. A simple plan, however, means you order only the food you need, and nothing is wasted.
- Agree to a total amount that you feel happy spending on food each week. If you're shopping together, take into account that not everyone will have the same budget or priorities.
- Once a month, buy nonperishable items, such as toilet paper, breakfast cereal, cleaning products, and canned goods in bulk; in general, you'll save money by buying these groceries in bigger quantities.
- You don't have to just shop in one supermarket; become savings savvy by shopping around to find the best deals.
- Some supermarkets offer coupons or discounts; if these are items you'd normally buy, stock up while the prices are good.
- If there's an incredible offer on a certain ingredient, you can change your recipe plan—flexibility is key.

ESSENTIAL EQUIPMENT

You don't need a kitchen fit for a photo shoot or equipped like a professional restaurant, in order to rustle up a decent meal. In fact, it's better to keep things simple—stick to essential utensils and implements so you don't clutter up cupboards and end up with more dish washing than needs to be done. Here's a list of the basics that will see you through every recipe in the book.

Utensils

- Liquid measuring cup
- Measuring cups and spoons
- Mixing bowls (1 small, 1 large)
- 2 wooden spoons
- Rolling pin
- Grater
- Spatula
- Cutting boards
- Vegetable peeler
- Wire balloon whisk and/or handheld mixer
- 2 sharp knives (1 small, 1 large)

Pots and pans

- 3 saucepans (large, medium, and small, with lids)
- Skillet
- Colander (metal so it can also be used as a steamer)

Cookware

- Metal baking sheets
- Wire cooling rack
- Ovenproof dishes
- Casserole dish
- Muffin pan
- Loaf pan
- Toaster

Staying healthy

Leaving home and fending for yourself can be something of a shock to the system. As well as navigating a new town or city, finding your way around campus and taking charge of your own washing, cooking, and cleaning, it's also important to look after your health. Late nights socializing and long days studying (yes, you need to do that, too) don't always leave a lot of time to plan for healthy meals and exercise. But your body and brain will only function well if you eat a balanced diet and get regular exercise. Halls of residence and shared student houses are also breeding grounds for germs, so anything you can do to boost your immune system will help you to fight off any winter colds or bouts of flu that are doing the rounds.

Eat your greens—The more the better, so try to eat up to ten portions of fresh fruit and vegetables every day to stay in tip-top condition. Snack on fruit during the day, add salad to your lunch, and steam plenty of fresh vegetables for dinner.

Run riot—You don't need to join a gym or pay for expensive fitness classes to keep in shape. You can take up running, work out at home, or offer your services as a dog walker (and earn some cash in the process) to make sure you get regular exercise.

Steer away from colds—Easier said than done, but if you see your housemates dropping like flies from some nasty virus or the dreaded flu, consider escaping back home for a couple of days until the contagious period has passed.

Clean it up—Students are not generally known for their high standards of hygiene in the kitchen. And while you might be a stickler for a disinfected surface, your housemates and visiting friends might not be as worried about germs clustering on dirty dishcloths and colonies of bacteria growing in unwashed coffee mugs. Wash cloths and dish towels regularly, wipe down surfaces with disinfectant, and use antiseptic hand wash.

Food hygiene—As a vegan, you'll avoid a number of obvious food-related issues in the kitchen, but there are still plenty of ways to make yourself ill if you're not careful, and wilted greens can harbor just as many potential bugs as a piece of chicken. Always completely defrost food before using it; do not reheat cooked food more than once (and check that it is piping hot all the way through); consume food by the expiration date; and put any leftovers in the refrigerator or freezer as soon as cool enough to transfer.

THE VEGAN PANTRY

Whether you have a shelf or a whole cupboard to store your food, there are certain ingredients that you should always keep in stock. You can buy many of these ingredients in bulk and save money as long as you have the space to store them. However, fresh fruit, vegetables, tofu, and meat and cheese replacements should be bought often and in smaller amounts, so you don't waste food.

Oil—Olive, sunflower, canola, and coconut oil are all good options, because you can use them in a wide range of dishes.

Onions and garlic—You'll use these often, so keep a good stock in a cool, dry place. For emergencies, garlic paste is a pretty good substitute for fresh garlic and doesn't require peeling and chopping.

Tofu—Store fresh tofu in the refrigerator, where it will keep for 3–5 days.

Nuts and seeds—From cashew nuts in stir-fry and curry dishes, to pistachios and pumpkin seeds for healthy daytime snacks, aim to keep a good selection of nuts and seeds in your cupboard.

Pasta—Egg-free lasagne, spaghetti, penne, and macaroni are good staples to have on permanent standby.

Noodles—Egg-free noodles make a quick and easy stir-fry dinner. Choose from dry or canned types, both of which have long shelf lives.

Rice—Whole-grain brown rice is more nutritious but basmati or long-grain rice is delicious served with Indian dishes, and risotto rice is essential for an Italian supper.

Grains—Couscous, bulgur wheat, quinoa, and cornmeal are all hearty grains that will make a meal in themselves, or they can be served as a side dish, used in salads, or added to soups and stews.

Beans (legumes)—Cans of chickpeas (garbanzo beans) are handy for stews, as well as lentils (green and red) and split peas for lasagne, pasta sauces, and soups.

Herbs and spices—A good selection of dried spices and herbs is the secret to delicious food. Start with chili, paprika, turmeric, mustard seeds, cumin, cilantro, tarragon, and oregano. Try to buy fresh herbs, wherever possible for sauces, salads, and garnishes.

Diced tomatoes—Inexpensive and nutritious, these can be used in everything from parmigiana to pizza toppings.

Coconut milk—Rich and creamy, this is an essential ingredient in many Thai and Indian dishes, as well as soups, cakes, and desserts.

Baked beans—Beans on toast can be an easy, inexpensive lunch. Plus, they're great for filling baked potatoes or for adding to a chili.

KICK OFF THE DAY

RAW FRESH GINGER & OAT BARS

TOASTED MUESLI WITH
COCONUT CHIPS

MUSHROOM RISOTTO CAKES

FLATBREAD, ROASTED VEG
& HUMMUS

PEACH & GINGER
Juice

2 peaches
1 inch piece of fresh ginger root,
    peeled and coarsely chopped
ice cubes
sparkling mineral water
mint leaves, to serve

Serves **1**
Prep time **10 minutes**

1 Halve the peaches and remove the pits. Juice the peaches with the chopped ginger.

2 Pour the juice into a tall glass over ice, add a splash of sparkling mineral water and a couple of mint leaves, and serve immediately.

VARIATION

For grapefruit fizz, juice 1 grapefruit with 1 cucumber and the juice of 1/2 a lemon. Top off with sparkling mineral water and stir in some chopped mint.

AFFORDABILITY 1

WATERMELON
& RASPBERRY
JUICE

1 wedge watermelon
   (2 cups when prepared)
1 cup raspberries
2-3 ice cubes

Serves **1**
Prep time **10 minutes**

1 Halve the melon and seed. Scoop out the flesh and cut into cubes. Juice the melon with the raspberries.

2 Pour into a glass, add a couple of ice cubes, and serve immediately.

VARIATION
For watermelon & orange juice, juice 2 oranges with the melon instead of the raspberries.

BEET & BERRY *Smoothie*

1 small beet
²⁄₃ cup blueberries, plus extra to
   serve (optional)
¾ cup raspberries
2–3 ice cubes

Serves **1**
Prep time **10 minutes**

1 Juice the beet in a food processor or blender.

2 Add the blueberries, raspberries, and ice cubes and process until smooth.

3 Pour the mixture into a glass, decorate with blueberries, if liked, and serve immediately.

AFFORDABILITY
1

STUDENT TIP

SMOOTHIE BOOST Keep a stock of berries in the freezer for an instant morning smoothie. Combine with nondairy milk and a handful of oats for a filling breakfast on the go.

ROASTED GRANOLA

5 tablespoons agave syrup
2 tablespoons sunflower oil
3 cups rolled oats
⅓ cup hazelnuts, coarsely
chopped
⅓ cup blanched almonds,
coarsely chopped
⅓ cup dried cranberries
⅓ cup dried blueberries

Serves **4**
Prep time **10 minutes,
plus cooling**
Cooking time **25-30 minutes**

1 Heat the agave syrup and oil together gently in a small saucepan.

2 Mix the oats and nuts together thoroughly in a large bowl. Pour over the syrup mixture and stir well to combine.

3 Spread the mixture over a large nonstick baking sheet and bake in a preheated oven, at 300°F, for 20-25 minutes, stirring once, until golden.

4 Let the granola cool, then stir in the dried berries. Serve with soy yogurt and fresh fruit. Any remaining granola can be stored in an airtight container.

AFFORDABILITY 1

RAW FRESH GINGER & OAT BARS

1. Line an 8½ × 3½ inch cake pan or similar-size container with plastic wrap.

2. Put the ginger, tahini, and 1¼ cups of the prunes into a food processor and process until smooth.

3. Add the oats, buckwheat, and 3 tablespoons of the sesame seeds, and process again until combined. Add the golden raisins and pulse briefly.

4. Turn the dough into the prepared pan and press down firmly in an even layer.

5. Wipe out the processor and process the remaining prunes and the apple juice until you have a smooth paste.

6. Spread the filling over the oat and buckwheat layer and sprinkle with the remaining sesame seeds. Lift out of the pan and serve cut into bars.

2 inch piece of fresh ginger root, grated
2½ tablespoons tahini
2 cups pitted prunes
1 cup rolled oats
2 ⅔ cups buckwheat flakes
¼ cup sesame seeds
⅔ cup golden raisins
¼ cup apple juice

Makes **16**
Prep time **10 minutes,
    plus soaking**

TOASTED MUESLI
with coconut chips

4⅓ cups rolled oats
1 cup coconut chips
½ cup sunflower seeds
1½ cups pumpkin seeds
1½ cups slivered almonds
¾ cup hazelnuts
¼ cup maple syrup
2 tablespoons sunflower oil
1⅔ cups golden raisins
9 dried figs, coarsely chopped

To serve
soy milk
raspberries

Serves **8**
Prep time **15 minutes**
Cooking time **15-20 minutes**

1 Mix together the oats, coconut chips, sunflower and pumpkin seeds, slivered almonds, and hazelnuts in a large bowl.

2 Transfer half the muesli mixture to a separate bowl. Mix the maple syrup and sunflower oil together in a bowl, then pour it over the remaining half of the muesli and toss really well to lightly coat all the ingredients.

3 Line a large roasting pan with parchment paper, sprinkle with the syrup-coated muesli, and spread out in a single layer. Bake in a preheated oven, at 300°F, for 15-20 minutes, stirring occasionally, until golden and crisp.

4 Let cool completely, then toss with the uncooked muesli and the golden raisins and figs. Store in an airtight storage jar. Serve with soy milk and raspberries.

VARIATION
For soft cinnamon muesli with almonds & banana, mix together 4⅓ cups olled oats, 1⅔ cups golden raisins, 1½ cups pumpkin seeds, 1⅓ cups toasted blanched almonds, 1 cup soft dried banana slices, ½ cup each pitted dried dates and sunflower seeds, and 2 teaspoons ground cinnamon in a large bowl. Store in an airtight storage jar. Serve with soy milk or soy yogurt and fresh fruit, if liked.

AFFORDABILITY 1

APRICOT & FRESH GINGER MUFFINS

1²/₃ cups all-purpose flour
3¾ teaspoons baking powder
1¼ cups chopped dried apricots
1¼ cups rolled oats, plus
    extra to sprinkle
²/₃ cup sugar
finely grated zest and juice
    of 1 large orange
¹/₃ cup peeled and finely chopped
    fresh ginger root
½ cup oat milk
½ cup vegetable oil
    or mild olive oil

Makes **12**
Prep time **10 minutes**
Cooking time **20 minutes**

1 Line a 12-cup muffin pan with paper muffin liners. Sift the flour and baking powder into a bowl and stir in the apricots, oats, and sugar.

2 In a separate bowl, combine the orange zest and juice, ginger, oat milk, and oil. Mix well and add to the dry ingredients.

3 Using a large metal spoon, stir the ingredients together until they're only just combined. Spoon into the muffin liners and sprinkle with extra oats.

4 Bake in a preheated oven, at 400°F, for 18–20 minutes, until the muffins have risen and golden. Serve warm or cold. Any leftover muffins will freeze well - just warm through before serving.

AFFORDABILITY **1**

STUDENT TIP

STAY HYDRATED A busy student life means it's easy to forget to drink enough water. Drink a glass as soon as you get up and keep a bottle in your bag and refill it during the day.

CARROT & APPLE *Muffins*

1 Line a 12-cup muffin pan with paper liners or lightly oil and line the bottoms with disks of parchment paper.

2 Sift the flour, baking powder, baking soda, salt, cinnamon, and ginger together into a bowl. Stir in the raisins, sugar, and poppy seeds.

3 Mix the almond milk, oi,l and vinegar together in a bowl. Add to the dry ingredients and lightly stir together until just mixed. Quickly fold in the apple and carrot, then divide the mixture among the paper liners or the cups of the muffin pan.

4 Bake immediately in a preheated oven, at 375°F, for 15-20 minutes, until well risen and golden. Transfer to a wire rack to cool. Store the muffins for up to for 2-3 days in an airtight container, or freeze.

2⅓ cups all-purpose flour
2¼ teaspoons baking powder
1½ teaspoons baking soda
½ teaspoon salt
1½ teaspoons ground cinnamon
1 teaspoon ground ginger
½ cup raisins
150 g (5 oz) light muscovado sugar
1 tablespoon poppy seeds
1 cup plus 2 tablespoons almond milk
½ cup olive oil, plus extra for oiling (optional)
1 tablespoon apple cider vinegar
1 sweet, firm apple, cored and coarsely grated
1 carrot, peeled and shredded

Makes **12**
Prep time **20 minutes**
Cooking time **15-20 minutes**

AFFORDABILITY
1

BLUEBERRY & VANILLA
FRENCH TOAST

1 teaspoon cornstarch
1/3 cup oat milk
1 tablespoon sugar, plus extra for
  sprinkling
1/2 teaspoon vanilla extract
2 chunky slices of white or seeded
  vegan bread
1 tablespoon dairy-free spread
1 tablespoon vegetable oil
1/2 cup blueberries
soy yogurt, to serve (optional)

Serves **2**
Prep time **5 minutes**
Cooking time **5 minutes**

1 Put the cornstarch into a small bowl and gradually blend in the milk until smooth. Add the sugar and vanilla extract and pour into a shallow bowl.

2 Turn both bread slices in the flavored milk until it is evenly absorbed.

3 Heat the dairy-free spread and oil in a skillet until bubbling. Cook the bread slices, one at a time if they don't both fit, for about 2 minutes, until golden on the underside. Turn with a spatula to brown the other side.

4 Transfer to plates and add the blueberries to the pan. Heat briefly to warm through and spoon onto the bread. Serve sprinkled with extra sugar and soya yogurt, if liked.

AFFORDABILITY
1

HOME-BAKED BEANS *on toast*

1 Soak the beans in plenty of cold water overnight. Drain, transfer to a saucepan, and cover with cold water.

2 Bring to a boil, then drain and return to the pan. Cover with fresh cold water, bring to a boil, and boil for 10 minutes, then cover and simmer for 50 minutes, until tender.

3 Meanwhile, heat the oil in a separate saucepan, add the red onion, and cook for 3 minutes, until just starting to soften.

4 Add the tomatoes, tomato paste, sugar, vinegar, paprika, dry mustard, and broth. Bring to a boil, stirring, then reduce the heat and simmer, uncovered, for 20 minutes, until reduced slightly.

5 Drain the cooked beans and add to the tomato sauce. Simmer for another 15–20 minutes, covered, until the sauce has thickened.

6 Season with salt and pepper and serve on whole-wheat toast, sprinkled with the chopped parsley.

1²/₃ cups dried navy beans
2 tablespoons canola oil
1 red onion, cut into wedges
1 (14½ oz) can diced tomatoes
2 tablespoons tomato paste
2 tablespoons packed dark
  brown sugar
3 tablespoons vegan
  red wine vinegar
1 teaspoon paprika
1 teaspoon dry mustard
1 cup vegetable broth
  (see page 219)
salt and pepper
2 tablespoons chopped flat leaf
  parsley, to garnish
whole-wheat toast, to serve

Serves **4**
Prep time **10 minutes,**
  plus overnight soaking
Cooking time **1 hour 20 minutes**

FEELING FIT

Being healthy isn't just about eating a well-balanced diet; you also need to get regular exercise. This boosts your endorphins (the happy chemicals in your brain), helps to keep you alert, gets your blood pumping, and keeps your immune system on top form.

If you already participate in a sport, it should be easy enough to join a club or find a local team you can train with. But, if you're not a natural gym bunny, it might mean a lifestyle change to incorporate exercise into your daily routine. And there are plenty of opportunities to pull on your tracksuit and work up a sweat without going anywhere near a baseball field, basketball court, or a gym.

WORKOUT DVD OR APP

There are literally hundreds of these on the market, from famous fitness gurus to svelte celebrities, demonstrating their favorite exercises for dropping a few pounds. Involve your housemates and get belly busting in the living room, or keep it quiet and practice your yoga moves in your bedroom.

COUNT YOUR STEPS

Use an app or buy a cheap pedometer and set yourself the 10,000 steps a day challenge (or 20,000 if you're feeling ambitious). If you walk to college or live on a large campus, it shouldn't be too much extra exertion to reach the target.

RENT A DOG
Or borrow one, to be more accurate. There are a few websites that link up lonely dogs with people who'd love a dog but can't keep one at home. If you're an animal lover looking for regular exercise, this could be the ideal solution.

TAKE THE STAIRS
If your college and/or accomodations are multistory, walking up stairs (or running when you want a real challenge) is a great way to burn calories and build muscle. No special equipment is required and no one will have a clue that you're working out instead of running late.

TAKE TO TWO WHEELS
How about getting fit and earning money at the same time? There are on-demand jobs for bicycle messengers and delivery people in urban areas, and you can work hours that don't interfere with lectures.

WEIGH IT UP
Whether it's a set of dumbbells or a couple of cans of beans, lifting weights is fun and will give you some muscle definition. It's a cheap, easy workout that will give you a well-earned break from writing essays or studying.

Mushroom
TOFU SCRAMBLE

1 Heat the oil in a skillet, add the mushrooms, and cook over high heat, stirring frequently, for 2 minutes, until browned and softened.

2 Add the tofu and cook, stirring, for 1 minute.

3 Add the tomatoes to the pan and cook for 2 minutes, until starting to soften.

4 Stir in the mushroom ketchup and half the parsley and season with salt and pepper.

5 Serve immediately with hash browns, sprinkled with the remaining parsley.

VARIATION

For spinach & corn tofu scramble, heat 2 tablespoons canola or olive oil in a skillet. Add 8 oz firm tofu, drained, patted dry, and crumbled, with 1 teaspoon smoked paprika and cook, stirring, for 2 minutes, until hot. Add $1/2$ cup frozen or drained canned corn kernels and heat through for 1 minute, then add 2 (4 oz) packages spinach and heat until just wilted. Season with salt and pepper and serve with hash browns or toasted sourdough bread.

2 tablespoons canola or olive oil
3 cups trimmed and quartered cremini mushrooms
8 oz firm tofu, drained, patted dry and crumbled
1 cup baby plum tomatoes, halved
1 tablespoon mushroom ketchup
3 tablespoons chopped flat leaf parsley
salt and pepper
hash browns, to serve

Serves **4**
Prep time **15 minutes**
Cooking time **5 minutes**

Creamy MUSHROOMS WITH WALNUTS

1 tablespoon olive oil

2½ cups trimmed and sliced cremini mushrooms

1 garlic clove, crushed

2 sprigs of thyme, plus extra to garnish

⅔ cup soy or oat cream

1 teaspoon soy sauce

½ cup chopped walnuts, toasted pepper

bagels, halved and toasted

Serves **2**

Prep time **10 minutes**

Cooking time **8 minutes**

1 Heat the oil in a skillet, add the mushrooms, and cook over high heat, stirring frequently, for 2 minutes, until browned and softened.

2 Reduce the heat and add the garlic, thyme, soy or oat cream, and soy sauce. Simmer, stirring, for 3 minutes, adding a little water if the sauce is too thick.

3 Stir in the walnuts and season with pepper (the soy sauce is salty, so you won't need to season with salt).

4 Spoon the mushroom mixture over the toasted bagels and garnish with thyme sprigs before serving.

AFFORDABILITY
1

MUSHROOM
Risotto cakes

1 Heat the olive oil in a large, heavy skillet, add the onion, leek, mushrooms, and garlic and cook over medium-high heat for 5-6 minutes, until softened and golden.

2 Add the rice and stir well, then add the broth, reduce the heat to a gentle simmer, and cook, stirring frequently, until the liquid is almost all absorbed and the rice is tender and cooked through, adding more broth, if necessary.

3 Remove from the heat and let cool for 20 minutes. The mixture will not only cool but more liquid will be absorbed and the rice will become a little more stodgy.

4 Divide the mixture into 8 and mold each portion into a large patty. Toss liberally in the cornmeal and set aside.

5 Heat the sunflower oil in a skillet and cook the cakes over medium-high heat for 2-3 minutes on each side, until golden and crisp. Serve hot with a simple dressed salad.

VARIATION

For butternut squash risotto cakes, cook the onion and leek over medium-high heat as above with 1 1/2 cups peeled, seeded, and finely chopped butternut squash pieces in place of the mushrooms. Reduce the heat, cover, and cook for another 3-4 minutes. Remove the lid, add the rice, and continue as above. Serve the cakes with a simple salad.

3 tablespoons olive oil
1 red onion, finely chopped
1 leek, trimmed, cleaned, and
    thinly sliced
4 cups trimmed and coarsely
    chopped cremini mushrooms
1 garlic clove, crushed
1 cup risotto rice
3 cups vegetable broth (see page
    219), plus extra if needed
1/2 cup cornmeal
1/4 cup sunflower oil

Serves **4**
Prep time **20 minutes,**
    plus cooling
Cooking time **25 minutes**

Flatbread, ROASTED VEG & HUMMUS

1²/₃ cups whole-wheat flour,
    plus extra for dusting
½ teaspoon salt
1 red bell pepper, cored,
    seeded, and cut into chunks
1 orange bell pepper, cored,
    seeded, and cut into chunks
1 green beel pepper, cored,
    seeded, and cut into chunks
1 large red onion, cut into thin
    wedges
2 tablespoons olive oil
½ teaspoon ground coriander
½ teaspoon cumin seeds

Hummus
1 (15 oz) can chickpeas
    (garbanzo beans), drained
finely grated zest and juice of
    1 lemon
3 tablespoons chopped parsley
1 tablespoon tahini
3 tablespoons olive oil
salt and pepper

Serves **4**
Prep time **20 minutes,
    plus standing**
Cooking time **20 minutes**

1 Preheat the oven to 425°F.

2 Mix the flour and salt together in a bowl, then add enough water to bring the mixture together into a dough—about 7-8 tablespoons. Turn out onto a lightly floured surface and knead well until smooth. Return to the bowl, cover with plastic wrap, and let rest in a warm place for 30 minutes.

3 Toss thebell peppers and onion with the oil in a large roasting pan, then add the coriander and cumin and toss again. Roast for 20 minutes, until softened.

4 Meanwhile, blend together all the ingredients for the hummus in a blender or food processor until smooth.

5 Divide the flatbread dough into 4 pieces and roll out each into a 10 inch round.

6 Heat a large skillet until hot and cook the flatbreads for about 45 seconds on each side, until lightly golden, flipping them over with a spatula.

7 Spread each warm flatbread with some of the hummus, then top with one-quarter of the hot roasted vegetables and fold to serve.

AFFORDABILITY
1

HEARTY BREAKFAST QUARTET

1 Cook the potatoes in boiling water for 5 minutes to soften; drain well.

2 Remove as much excess water from the tofu as you can by squeezing it between layers of paper towels. Cut into 1/4 inch thick slices and press between additional layers of paper towels to remove any remaining moisture. Combine the paprika, salt, cumin, and mint on a plate. Turn the tofu slices in the mixture to coat.

3 Coarsely grate the potato into a bowl and stir in the oregano and a little salt and pepper. Shape into small cakes by packing the mixture, half at a time, into a small metal cookie cutter, about 3 1/2 inches in diameter. If you don't have one, press the mixture into 2 small patty shapes with your hands.

4 Heat 1 tablespoon of the oil in a skillet. Add the mushrooms and potato cakes and cook gently for about 5 minutes, turning with a spatula until the mushrooms are tender and the potatoes are golden. Add the tomatoes and cook briefly to soften. Lift out onto serving plates and keep warm.

5 Heat the remaining oil in the pan and cook the tofu for about 2 minutes on each side, until golden. Transfer to the plates and sprinkle with parsley and a drizzle of any juices left in the pan.

10 oz small Yukon gold potatoes, scrubbed and cut into small chunks
7 oz tofu
1/2 teaspoon smoked paprika
1/2 teaspoon salt
1/4 teaspoon ground cumin
1/4 teaspoon dried mint
1/4 teaspoon dried oregano
3 tablespoons mild olive oil or vegetable oil
2 large portobello mushrooms
2 tomatoes, halved
salt and pepper
chopped parsley, to sprinkle

Serves **2**
Prep time **15 minutes**
Cooking time **15 minutes**

SOUPS, SALADS, SIDES & SNACKS

CORN, TOMATO & BLACK BEAN SALAD

SEEDED FRIES WITH RED PEPPER DIP.

ONION, TOMATO &
CHICKPEA SOUP

2 tablespoons olive oil
2 red onions, coarsely chopped
2 garlic cloves, finely chopped
2 teaspoons packed brown sugar
5 tomatoes (about 1¼ lb), skinned
   if liked, coarsely chopped
2 teaspoons harissa paste
3 teaspoons tomato paste
1 (15 oz) can chickpeas (garbanzo
   beans), drained and rinsed
3¾ cups vegetable broth
   (see page 219)
salt and pepper

Serves **6**
Prep time **15 minutes**
Cooking time **1 hour 10 minutes**

AFFORDABILITY

1

1 Heat the oil in a large saucepan, add the onions, and sauté over low heat for 10 minutes, stirring occasionally, until just beginning to brown around the edges. Stir in the garlic and sugar and cook for another 10 minutes, stirring more frequently as the onions begin to caramelize.

2 Stir in the tomatoes and harissa paste and cook for 5 minutes. Mix in the tomato paste, chickpeas, broth, and salt and pepper and bring to a boil. Cover and simmer for 45 minutes, until the tomatoes and onion are soft. Taste and adjust the seasoning, if needed.

3 Ladle into bowls and serve with warm ciabatta.

VARIATION
For spicy red onion & bean soup, make up the soup as above but omit the harissa and add 1 teaspoon of smoked paprika and 1 split dried red chili when cooking the tomatoes, then swap the chickpeas for the same size can of red kidney beans. Serve with warm ciabatta.

BEET & APPLE *Soup*

1 tablespoon olive oil
1 tablespoon dairy-free spread
2 cooking apples, such as Granny
   Smith, peeled, cored, and
   chopped
1 sweet, crisp apple, such as
   Pink Lady or Pippin, peeled,
   cored, and chopped
12 cooked beets (about 1¼ lb),
   coarsely chopped
2 teaspoons caraway seeds
4–5 sprigs of thyme
6⅓ cups vegetable broth
   (see page 219)
salt and pepper
plain soy yogurt, to serve
chopped dill, to garnish

Serves **4**
Prep time **10 minutes**
Cooking time **10 minutes**

1 Heat the oil and vegan spread in a large saucepan and sauté the apples for 2–3 minutes, until golden. Add the cooked beets, caraway seeds, and thyme and stir-fry for 1–2 minutes.

2 Add the vegetable broth, bring to a boil, then cook for 10 minutes.

3 In a blender or with a handheld blender, process the soup until fairly smooth, and season to taste.

4 Serve in bowls with soy yogurt swirled through. Garnish with chopped dill and freshly ground black pepper.

AFFORDABILITY 1

Chilled
GAZPACHO

1. Mix together the vegetables, garlic, chili, and cilantro or flat leaf parsley in a large bowl.

2. Add the vinegar, tomato paste, oil, and a little salt. Process in batches in a food processor or blender until smooth, scraping the mixture down from the sides of the bowl, if necessary.

3. Put the blended mixture into a clean bowl and check the seasoning, adding a little more salt, if needed. Chill for up to 24 hours before serving.

4. To serve, ladle the gazpacho into large bowls, sprinkle with ice cubes, and garnish with parsley or cilantro, cucumber, bell pepper, and onion.

VARIATION

For chilled couscous gazpacho, prepare the soup as above, omitting the red bell peppers, and chill. Put ¼ cup couscous into a bowl and pour in just enough boiling water to come to ½ inch above the level of the couscous. Cover with plastic wrap and set aside for 10 minutes. Uncover, break the couscous up with a fork, and let cool to room temperature. Stir into the soup with the chopped herbs just before serving along with a little harissa on the side. Omit the ice and garnishes.

AFFORDABILITY 1

7 tomatoes (about 1¾ lb), skinned and coarsely chopped
½ cucumber, coarsely chopped
2 red bell peppers, cored, seeded, and coarsely chopped
1 celery stalk, chopped
2 garlic cloves, chopped
½ red chili, seeded and sliced
small handful of cilantro or flat leaf parsley
2 tablespoons vegan white wine vinegar
2 tablespoons tomato paste
¼ cup olive oil
salt

To serve
ice cubes
flat-leaf parsley or cilantro, finely chopped
finely diced cucumber, bell pepper, and onion

Serves **6**
Prep time **20 minutes, plus chilling**

LIMA BEAN & VEGETABLE *Soup*

1 tablespoon olive oil
2 teaspoons smoked paprika
1 celery stalk, sliced
2 carrots, sliced
1 leek, trimmed, cleaned and sliced
2½ cups vegetable broth
  (see page 219)
1 (14½ oz) can diced tomatoes
1 (15 oz) can lima beans, drained
  and rinsed
2 teaspoons chopped rosemary
salt and pepper

Serves **4**
Prep time **10 minutes**
Cooking time **25 minutes**

1 Heat the oil in a large saucepan, add the paprika, celery, carrots, and leek, and cook over medium heat for 3-4 minutes, until the vegetables are slightly softened.

2 Pour in the broth and tomatoes and add the lima beans and rosemary. Season to taste with salt and pepper and bring to a boil, then cover and simmer for 15 minutes or until the vegetables are just tender.

3 Ladle into warm bowls and sprinkle with freshly ground black pepper.

AFFORDABILITY
1

STUDENT TIP

PANTRY STAPLES Keep your cupboards well stocked with essentials, such as beans, rice, pasta, and diced tomatoes so that when the budget is looking a little tight toward the end of the month, you'll always be able to rustle up a reasonable meal.

STANDBY
SPICY BEAN
SOUP

1 Heat the vegetable oil in a large, heavy saucepan or flameproof casserole dish and sauté the onion and bell pepper over medium-high heat for 4 minutes. Add the garlic and cook for another 2 minutes, until lightly browned.

2 Stir in the spice mix, then add half the kidney beans and half the black beans, all of the diced tomatoes, measured water, and bouillon cube. Stir well, bring to a boil, and simmer for 10-12 minutes, until slightly thickened.

3 Use a handheld blender to blend the soup until almost smooth, then stir in the remaining beans and heat through. Ladle into 4 deep bowls and serve immediately with a drizzle of plain soy yogurt and a sprinkling of tortilla chips.

2 tablespoons vegetable oil
1 large onion, chopped
1 red bell pepper, cored, seeded, and chopped
2 garlic cloves, chopped
¼ oz cup Mexican fajita or taco spice mix
1 (15 oz) can kidney beans, drained and rinsed
1 (15 oz) can black beans, drained and rinsed
1 (14½ oz) can diced tomatoes
3 cups boiling water
1 vegetable bouillon cube

To serve
¼ cup plain soy yogurt
1 cup tortilla chips (optional)

Serves **4**
Prep time **10 minutes**
Cooking time **20 minutes**

AFFORDABILITY
1

BUTTERNUT SOUP
with peanut pesto

2 tablespoons olive oil
1 onion, finely chopped
1 butternut squash (about 1¾ lb), peeled, seeded, and cut into chunks
1²/₃ cups coconut milk
1 tablespoon vegan Thai green curry paste
2½ cups vegetable broth (see page 219)

Pesto

1 green chili, seeded and finely chopped
2 tablespoons unsalted peanuts, coarsely chopped
¼ cup chopped cilantro
½ inch piece of fresh ginger root, peeled and grated
1 tablespoon olive oil
salt and pepper

Serves **6**
Prep time **20 minutes**
Cooking time **40 minutes**

1 Mix all the ingredients for the pesto together in a small serving bowl and season with a little salt and plenty of pepper. Set aside.

2 Heat the oil in a large, heavy saucepan, add the onion and butternut squash, and cook over medium-high heat for 5–6 minutes, until softened and golden in places.

3 Add the coconut milk, curry paste, and broth and bring to a boil, stirring constantly. Cover and simmer gently for 30 minutes, until the squash is tender.

4 Transfer the soup, in batches, to a blender or food processor and blend until smooth. Return to the pan and reheat.

5 Ladle into warm serving bowls, spoon a little of the pesto over the top, and swirl through.

BLACK BEAN SOUP
WITH SOBA NOODLES

1. Cook the noodles in a large saucepan of boiling water for about 5 minutes, or according to the package directions, until just tender.

2. Meanwhile, heat the oil in a saucepan over medium heat, add the scallions and garlic, and stir-fry for 1 minute. Add the chili, ginger, black bean sauce, and broth and bring to a boil.

3. Stir the bok choy or spring greens, soy sauce, sugar, and peanuts into the soup, then reduce the heat and simmer gently for 4 minutes.

4. Drain the noodles, rinse with fresh hot water, and spoon into 4 warm bowls. Ladle the soup over the top and serve immediately.

8 oz dried soba noodles
2 tablespoons peanut oil or vegetable oil
1 bunch of scallions, sliced
2 garlic cloves, coarsely chopped
1 red chili, seeded and sliced
1½ inch piece of fresh ginger root, peeled and grated
½ cup black bean sauce or black bean stir-fry sauce
3 cups vegetable broth (see page 219)
3 cups shredded bok choy or collard greens
2 teaspoons light soy sauce
1 teaspoon sugar
⅓ cup raw unsalted peanuts

Serves **4**
Prep time **10 minutes**
Cooking time **8 minutes**

AFFORDABILITY
2

CABBAGE & GINGER SOUP

5 cups vegetable broth
(see page 219)
6 cups coarsely chopped
napa cabbage
2 tablespoons finely chopped
fresh ginger root
2 star anise
2 tablespoons light soy sauce
½ teaspoon sesame oil
white pepper

Serves **4**
Prep time **10 minutes**
Cooking time **15 minutes**

1 Put the broth into a large saucepan and bring to a boil. Add the cabbage, ginger, and star anise to the broth, return to a boil, and cook for 10–12 minutes.

2 Remove from the heat and stir in the soy sauce and sesame oil, season with white pepper, and ladle into warm bowls to serve.

VARIATION

For stir-fried napa cabbage with ginger & garlic, remove and discard the outer leaves from ½ napa cabbage and cut into large pieces. Crush 3 garlic cloves with a large pinch of salt in a mortar with a pestle until coarsely ground. Heat a wok or large nonstick skillet over high heat, add 2 tablespoons of peanut oil, and heat until almost smoking. Add the garlic and 1 tablespoon of peeled and grated fresh ginger root, then immediately add the cabbage and stir-fry, moving the ingredients constantly to prevent the garlic from burning. Cook until the cabbage is heated through but still crunchy. Transfer to a warm serving plate and season with white pepper before serving.

AFFORDABILITY
1

CHILI MISO *Soup*

1 Put the miso paste, soy sauce, and broth into a large saucepan and bring to a boil. Reduce the heat, add the noodles and ginger, and simmer for 5 minutes.

2 Meanwhile, heat the oil in a wok or large skillet, add the chili, sugar snap peas, shallots, and baby corn, and stir-fry over medium-high heat for 5 minutes, until softened.

3 Transfer the vegetable mixture to the pan with the noodles, add the cilantro, and stir through. Serve in warm serving bowls, garnished with the scallions.

VARIATION

For miso soup with ramen bell peppers & tofu, prepare the miso broth as above, then add 6 oz dried ramen noodles in place of the thin rice noodles and simmer for 5 minutes. Heat 1 tablespoon of sesame oil in a wok or large skillet, add 1 red and 1 yellow bell pepper, cored, seeded, and thinly sliced, with 1 cup coarsely chopped sugar snap peas and stir-fry over medium-high heat for 5 minutes, until softened. Add 4 oz firm tofu, drained, patted dry, and cubed, and gently toss for a few seconds, then transfer the mixture to the pan with the broth and noodles. Stir through, then serve ladled into warm bowls.

2 tablespoons miso paste
1 tablespoon dark soy sauce
6 cups vegetable broth
   (see page 219)
5 oz dried thin rice noodles
1 inch piece of fresh ginger root,
   peeled and grated
1 tablespoon sesame oil
½ red Thai chili, seeded and
   finely chopped
3 cups sugar snap peas,
   diagonally sliced
2 shallots, finely chopped
8 baby corn, coarsely sliced
⅓ cup chopped cilantro
2 scallions, thinly sliced,
   to serve

Serves **4**
Prep time **20 minutes**
Cooking time **10 minutes**

AFFORDABILITY
2

Tapenade
BRUSCHETTA

1 small ciabatta loaf, cut into
12 slices
3 tablespoons olive oil
1 garlic clove, crushed
1 tablespoon chopped flat leaf
parsley
12 marinated sun-dried tomatoes
in oil, drained

Tapenade
1½ cups pitted black olives
1 garlic clove
small handful of flat leaf parsley
2 tablespoons capers
1 tablespoon lemon juice
2 tablespoons olive oil
salt and pepper

Makes **12**
Prep time **15 minutes**
Cooking time **10 minutes**

1 Arrange the ciabatta slices in a single layer on a baking sheet. Mix the oil, garlic, and chopped parsley together and brush over the bread slices.

2 Bake in a preheated oven, at 400°, for 10 minutes, until golden and crisp.

3 Meanwhile, put the olives, garlic, parsley, capers, lemon juice, and oil in a food processor and process to a coarse paste. Season with salt and pepper.

4 Spread the tapenade over the ciabatta toast and top each slice with a sun-dried tomato.

VARIATION
For artichoke tapenade bruschetta, toast the ciabatta slices as above. Meanwhile, put ¾ cup pitted green olives and 4 drained marinated artichokes in oil (reserving 2 tablespoons of the oil), a small handful of flat leaf parsley, 2 tablespoons of capers, 1 garlic clove, 1 tablespoon of lemon juice, and the reserved artichoke oil into a food processor and process to a coarse paste. Season with salt and pepper. Spread the tapenade over the toasts and sprinkle with chopped parsley.

AFFORDABILITY
1

Sweet OAT CAKES

3¼ cups cups rolled oats
⅓ cup sesame seeds
3 tablespoons poppy seeds
pinch of salt
½ cup boiling water
2 tablespoons agave syrup
½ cup extra virgin olive oil

Makes **20**
Prep time **15 minutes**
Cooking time **15 minutes**

1 Combine the rolled oats, sesame seeds, poppy seeds, and pinch of salt in a large bowl and make a well in the center.

2 Pour in a boiling water, agave syrup, and olive oil and stir with a wooden spoon to form a soft dough.

3 Shape the dough into 20 balls the size of a walnut. Put them onto a nonstick baking sheet and flatten them with the palm of your hand to make 3½ inch rounds.

4 Bake in a preheated oven, at 350°F, for about 15 minutes, until golden.

5 Remove the oat cakes from the oven and transfer to a wire rack to cool. Serve with vegan hard cheese and grapes.

AFFORDABILITY 1

STUDENT TIP

DON'T FORGET YOUR BAGS Always take a reusable shopping bag with you when leave the house to avoid adding to the landfill. Some states also have bans on single-use plastic bags and require a minimum charge for recycled or reusable bags.

SMOKY
TOFU NUGGETS
on toast

1 Preheat the oven to 350°F. Combine the soy sauce and avocado oil in a small bowl, then add the smoked tofu and mix well.

2 Spoon the tofu mixture onto an oiled baking sheet and place in the oven for 10-15 minutes or until crispy.

3 Heat the soy milk to just below boiling point. Add the canola oil and mix thoroughly with a handheld mixer. Add the vinegar, mixing all the time. Add the potato flour, mustard, tomato sauce, and bouillon powder to the milk mixture, mix again, and bring back to a boil, stirring constantly.

4 Spread the slices of bread with the yeast extract. Mix the baked tofu with the milk mixture, then spread on the bread.

5 Place the bread on the baking sheet and bake in the oven for 10 minutes, until golden and starting to bubble. Cut each slice into wedges, sprinkle with black pepper, and serve.

- 2 teaspoons soy sauce
- 2 teaspoons avocado oil or olive oil
- 2 oz smoked tofu or vegan bacon or ham, finely chopped
- ½ cup sweetened soy milk
- ½ cup canola oil
- 2 teaspoons apple cider vinegar
- 1 tablespoon potato flour
- 1 teaspoon English mustard
- 1 tablespoon vegan tomato sauce
- 1 teaspoon vegan bouillon powder
- 4 slices of whole-wheat bread
- 1 teaspoon yeast extract
- black pepper

Serves **2**
Prep time **10 minutes**
Cooking time **20-25 minutes**

AFFORDABILITY 2

Egg-free OMELET

1. Heat 1 tablespoon of olive oil in a large nonstick skillet with a lid, then gently sauté the onion, mushrooms, bell peppers, and tofu over medium heat for about 5 minutes, stirring occasionally.

2. Put the flour, baking powder, bouillon powder, milk, vinegar, mustard, soy sauce, herbes de Provence, 2 tablespoons of the remaining olive oil, and salt and pepper into a large bowl and whisk with a fork.

3. Fold in the soynnaise, then pour the mixture onto the vegetables in the skillet. Cook gently for 3-4 minutes with the pan covered so that the steam partly cooks the top.

4. Slide the omelet onto a plate, then oil the pan, place it upside down over the plate, and flip it over. Return the pan to the heat and brown the other side of the omelet. Serve hot with a mixed salad.

AFFORDABILITY
1

¼ cup olive oil
1 onion, chopped
6 mushrooms, sliced
½ red bell pepper, cored, seeded, and chopped
½ green bell pepper, cored, seeded, and chopped
2 oz tofu, crumbled
3 heaping tablespoons white bread flour
½ teaspoon baking powder
2 heaping teaspoons vegan bouillon powder
⅓ cup soy milk
1 tablespoon apple cider vinegar
1 teaspoon mustard
1 tablespoon soy sauce
2 teaspoons herbes de Provence
1 tablespoon Soynnaise (see page 218)
salt and pepper

Serves **2**
Prep time **10 minutes**
Cooking time **10 minutes**

ORANGE & AVOCADO *Salad*

4 large juicy oranges
2 small ripe avocados
2 teaspoons cardamom pods
3 tablespoons olive oil
1 tablespoon agave syrup
pinch of allspice
2 teaspoons lemon juice
salt and pepper
watercress or other peppery
  greens, to garnish

Serves **4**
Prep time **20 minutes**

1 Cut the skin and the white membrane off the oranges.
Working over a bowl to catch the juice, cut between the
membranes to remove the sections.

2 Peel and pit the avocados, slice the flesh, and toss gently with
the orange sections. Pile onto serving plates.

3 Reserve a few whole cardamom pods for garnishing. Crush
the remainder using a mortar and pestle to extract the seeds,
or put them into a small bowl and crush with the end of a
rolling pin. Pick out and discard the pods.

4 Mix the seeds with the oil, agave syrup, allspice, and lemon
juice. Season to taste with salt and pepper and stir in the
reserved orange juice.

5 Garnish the salad with watercress or other peppery greens
and the reserved cardamom pods and serve with the dressing
spooned over the top.

AFFORDABILITY
1

BROCCOLI, PEA & AVOCADO SALAD

1. Toast the sesame and chia seeds in a dry skillet over medium heat, shaking the pan a couple of times, for 30 seconds, until golden. Remove the seeds from the pan and let cool.

2. Blanch the broccoli with the peas in a large saucepan of boiling water for 2 minutes, until the broccoli is just tender but still firm. Drain, rinse under cold water, and drain again.

3. Transfer the broccoli and peas to a large salad bowl. Add the avocado, spinach leaves, alfalfa, if using, mint, and toasted seeds.

4. Whisk the lime juice, sesame oil, and ginger together in a bowl and season with salt and pepper. Pour the dressing over the salad and toss well to mix.

VARIATION

For spinach, beet & pomegranate salad, toast the sesame and chia seeds as above. Put 4 cups baby spinach leaves in a salad bowl with 1 cup chopped Sweet Fire beets (cooked beets infused with a sweet chii marinade), 2 sliced celery stalks, 1 large ripe avocado, peeled, pitted, and chopped, 1 cup alfalfa sprouts, a small handful of chopped flat leaf parsley leaves, and the toasted seeds. Make the lime juice dressing as above, then pour it over the salad and toss well to mix.

1 tablespoon sesame seeds
1 tablespoon chia seeds
1½ cups broccoli florets
1 cup frozen peas
1 large ripe avocado, peeled, pitted, and chopped
4 cups) baby spinach leaves
1 cup alfalfa sprouts (optional)
2 tablespoons chopped mint
juice of 1 lime
2 teaspoons sesame oil
¾ inch piece of fresh ginger root, peeled and grated
salt and pepper

Serves **4**
Prep time **20 minutes, plus cooling**
Cooking time **5 minutes**

AFFORDABILITY
1

CARROT & CASHEW NUT *Salad*

½ cup unsalted cashew nuts
2 tablespoons black mustard
  seeds
8 carrots, peeled and shredded
  (4½ cups prepared)
1 red bell pepper, cored, seeded,
  and thinly sliced
3 tablespoons chopped chervil
  or flat leaf parsley
2 scallions, thinly sliced

Dressing
2 tablespoons avocado oil
2 tablespoons raspberry vinegar
1 tablespoon whole-grain mustard
pinch of sugar
salt and pepper

Serves **4**
Prep time **10 minutes**
Cooking time **6-10 minutes**

1 Heat a dry nonstick skillet over medium-low heat and toast the cashew nuts, stirring frequently, for 5-8 minutes or until golden brown. Transfer the nuts to a small plate and let cool. Add the mustard seeds to the pan and toast them for 1-2 minutes or until they start to pop.

2 Mix together the mustard seeds, carrots, red bell pepper, chervil or parsley, and scallions in a large bowl.

3 Whisk together all the dressing ingredients in a small bowl, then pour the dressing onto the shredded carrot salad. Mix the salad thoroughly to coat and pile it into serving bowls.

4 Chop the cashew nuts coarsely and sprinkle them over the salad. Serve immediately.

COCONUT, CARROT & SPINACH SALAD

1 Put the spinach into a large bowl with the carrot and coconut, and toss together lightly.

2 Heat the oil a small skillet over medium heat. Add the mustard and cumin seeds and stir-fry for 20-30 seconds, until fragrant and the mustard seeds start to pop.

3 Remove from the heat and sprinkle the seeds over the salad. Pour the lime and orange juice over the top. Season well and toss before serving.

1 (10 oz) package baby spinach, finely chopped
1 carrot, peeled and shredded
⅓ cup grated fresh coconut
2 tablespoons peanut oil
2 teaspoons black mustard seeds
1 teaspoon cumin seeds
juice of 1 lime
juice of 1 orange
salt and pepper

Serves **4**
Prep time **10 minutes**
Cooking time **1 minute**

STUDENT TIP

DITCH THE BUS This obviously depends on how far away from campus you live, but it's easy to get your daily exercise quota by simply walking or cycling instead of relying on public transportation or a car. And you'll save money, too.

AFFORDABILITY
1

CHICKPEA & CHILI SALAD

2 (15 oz) cans chickpeas (garbanzo beans), drained and rinsed
2 plum tomatoes, coarsely chopped
4 scallions, thinly sliced
1 red chili, seeded and thinly sliced
¼ cup coarsely chopped cilantro leaves

Lemon dressing
2 tablespoons lemon juice
1 garlic clove, crushed
2 tablespoons olive oil
salt and pepper

To serve
toasted pita bread, cut into strips

Serves **4**
Prep time **10 minutes, plus 10 minutes standing**

1 Combine all the salad ingredients in a shallow bowl.

2 Put all the dressing ingredients into a screw-top jar, season to taste with salt and pepper, and shake well. Pour over the salad and toss well to coat all the ingredients.

3 Cover the salad and let stand at room temperature for about 10 minutes to let the flavors mingle. Serve with the toasted pita bread strips.

VARIATION
For white bean & sun-dried tomato salad, combine 2 (15 oz) cans cannellini (white kidney) beans, drained and rinsed, 1 cup drained and coarsely chopped sun-dried tomatoes in oil, 1 tablespoon of chopped and pitted black olives, 2 teaspoons of drained and rinsed capers, and 2 teaspoons of chopped thyme leaves. Toss in the lemon dressing and let stand as above, then serve with toasted slices of ciabatta bread.

AFFORDABILITY 1

CORN, TOMATO &
BLACK BEAN SALAD

4 ears of corn, shucked and silks
   removed
1¾ cups halved cherry tomatoes
1 (15 oz) can black beans, drained
   and rinsed
1 red onion, finely diced
1 avocado, peeled, pitted, and
   diced
small bunch of cilantro, coarsely
   chopped

Dressing
juice of 1 lime
2 tablespoons canola oil
2-3 drops Tabasco sauce

Serves **4**
Prep time **10 minutes**
Cooking time **10 minutes**

1 Cook the corn cobs in boiling water for 7-10 minutes. Cool
   briefly under running cold water, then slice off the kernels
   with a knife.

2 Put the kernels into a large bowl with the tomatoes, black
   beans, onion, and avocado and mix with the cilantro.

3 Make the dressing by mixing together the lime juice, oil, and
   Tabasco. Drizzle the dressing over the salad, stir carefully
   to combine, and serve immediately.

PACK YOUR LUNCH

A student budget can quickly disappear, with transportation costs, books and school supplies, coffees, evenings out with friends all adding up. So, if there's any way to cut costs, it can make a big difference to making your money last. Making your own lunch to take to college is quick and easy, and it could save you a small fortune over a semester or two. It will take some forward planning and maybe an earlier start, but it's worth it. The other bonus is you get to choose your lunch instead of being stuck with the solitary vegan-friendly selection at the counter.

COUSCOUS SALAD BOWL
Mix steamed and cooled couscous with chopped sun-dried tomatoes, olives, and chickpeas (garbanzo beans) and pack in a plastic storage container.

VEGETABLE WRAP
Fill a wrap with baby spinach, shredded carrot, grated beet, and cucumber sticks. Add a dollop of dairy-free pesto, vegan mayonnaise or Soynnaise (see page 218), roll it up ,and wrap in aluminum foil to keep fresh.

PASTA SALAD

The options are almost infinite when it comes to pasta. You can cook and cool enough pasta for two or three servings. Keep in an airtight container in the refrigerator and prepare a different lunch each day. Cherry tomatoes, basil, dairy-free pesto, pine nuts, steamed and cooled broccoli ,and peas are all easy additions.

GUACAMOLE

Mash an avocado with a little lime juice and a pinch of dried chili flakes for a delicious homemade dip. Pack in a small plastic storage container and take a pile of fresh breadsticks to scoop it up.

SOUP

Treat yourself to a thermos and enjoy hot soup during the winter. Make a big batch and it will keep in the refrigerator for two or three days. Chunky vegetable soups are filling and healthy, and by adding tiny pasta shapes, such as orzo, you can turn it into even more of a meal.

SANDWICH

There's nothing wrong with a simple sandwich for lunch, and making your own is much cheaper than buying them. Leafy greens, avocado slices, shredded,or sliced vegetables, plum tomatoes, vegan cheese, and some condiments or pickles will liven up your lunchtime.

BULGUR SALAD WITH ROASTED PEPPERS
on lettuce

AFFORDABILITY
1

1 Put the bulgur into a bowl, pour the measured boiling water over it, stir, then cover and let stand for 10-15 minutes until the grains are tender.

2 Add the tomato paste, lemon juice, olive oil, chili, and some salt to the bulgur mixture and mix thoroughly.

3 Add the roasted red peppers, scallions, and tomatoes, along with the parsley and mint, and mix well.

4 Arrange the lettuce around the edges of a platter with the bulgur salad in the center. Use the leaves to scoop up the bulgur mixture and eat.

1½ cups bulgur
½ cup boiling water
1 tablespoon tomato paste
juice of 1½ lemons
⅓ cup extra virgin olive oil
1 red chili, finely chopped
1 cup drained and diced roasted
   red peppers (from a jar)
8 scallions, thinly sliced
1⅔ cups diced tomatoes
1 cup coarsely chopped
   flat leaf parsley
⅔ cup coarsely chopped mint
4 boston lettuce, leaves separated
salt

Serves **4**
Prep time **30 minutes**

QUINOA, ZUCCHINI & POMEGRANATE SALAD

1 Cook the quinoa following the package directions, then drain and rinse under cold water. Drain again.

2 Cut the ends off the zucchini, then cut into ribbons using a potato peeler.

3 Whisk together the vinegar and 2 tablespoons of the oil in a bowl and season with salt and pepper.

4 Put the quinoa, zucchini ribbons, and remaining ingredients into a large bowl, pour over the dressing, and toss everything together and serve.

½ cup quinoa
1 large zucchini
1 tablespoon vegan white wine vinegar
¼ cup olive oil
4 scallions, thinly sliced
8 cherry tomatoes, halved
1 red chili, finely chopped
⅔ cup pomegranate seeds (or seeds of ½ pomegranate)
small handful of finely chopped flat leaf parsley
salt and pepper

Serves **4**
Prep time **20 minutes**

GINGERED TOFU
& MANGO SALAD

¼ cup peeled and grated fresh
   ginger root
2 tablespoons light soy sauce
1 garlic clove, finely chopped
1 tablespoon seasoned rice
   vinegar
4 oz firm silken tofu, cut into
   ½ inch cubes
2 tablespoons peanut oil or
   vegetable oil
1 bunch of scallions, sliced
   diagonally into ¾ inch lengths
⅓ cup cashew nuts
1 small mango, peeled, pitted,
   and sliced
½ small iceberg lettuce, shredded
2 tablespoons water

Serves **2**
Prep time **15 minutes,
   plus marinating**
Cooking time **5 minutes**

1 Mix together the ginger, soy sauce, garlic, and vinegar in a small bowl. Add the tofu to the bowl and toss the ingredients together. Let marinate for 15 minutes.

2 Lift the tofu from the marinade with a fork, drain, and reserve the marinade for later.

3 Heat the oil in a skillet over medium heat, add the tofu pieces, and gently cook for 3 minutes or until golden. Remove with a slotted spoon and keep warm. Add the scallions and cashew nuts to the pan and cook quickly for 30 seconds. Add the mango slices to the pan and cook for 30 seconds, or until heated through.

4 Pile the lettuce onto serving plates and sprinkle the tofu, scallions, mango, and cashew nuts over the top. Heat the marinade juices in the pan with the measured water, pour the mixture over the salad, and serve immediately.

VARIATION

For tofu & sugar snap salad, marinate and cook the tofu as above, reserving the marinade. Add the scallions and cashew nuts to the pan, also adding 1 red chili, thinly sliced, and 2 cups halved sugar snap peas. Omit the mango. Cook for 1 minute, until heated through, then gently toss in the fried tofu. Add the juice of ½ lime and 2 tablespoons of water to the reserved marinade and drizzle it over the salad before serving on the lettuce.

SOY TOFU SALAD
WITH CILANTRO

1 lb 2 oz firm tofu, drained and
cut into bite-size pieces
6 scallions, finely shredded
⅔ cup coarsely chopped cilantro
leaves
1 large mild red chili, seeded and
thinly sliced
¼ cup light soy sauce
2 teaspoons sesame oil

Serves **4**
Prep time **10 minutes,
plus standing**

1 Carefully arrange the tofu on a serving plate in a single layer.
Sprinkle the scallions, cilantro, and chilli over the top.

2 Drizzle with the soy sauce and oil, then let stand at room
temperature for 10 minutes before serving.

STUDENT TIP

USE YOUR SMARTPHONE From step counters
to shopping calculators and recipe planners, your
smartphone is so much more than a social media
hub. Use it to plan ahead, save money when you're
shopping, and to maintain a healthier lifestyle.

AFFORDABILITY
1

Fatoush SALAD

1 First make the dressing. Whisk the olive oil, lemon juice, garlic, and sumac together in a bowl. Season to taste.

2 To make the salad, combine the pita pieces, tomatoes, cucumber, radishes, red onion, lettuce, and mint in a large bowl.

3 When ready to serve, pour the dressing over the salad and gently mix together to coat the salad evenly.

VARIATION
For a Middle Eastern couscous salad, replace the pita bread with 2½ cups cooked couscous. Pour the dressing over the top, toss to mix well, and serve.

1 pita bread, torn into small pieces
6 plum tomatoes, seeded and coarsely chopped
½ cucumber, peeled and coarsely chopped
10 radishes, sliced
1 red onion, coarsely chopped
1 small boston lettuce, leaves separated
small handful of fresh mint leaves

Dressing
1 cup olive oil
juice of 3 lemons
1 garlic clove, crushed
2 teaspoons sumac (or ½ teaspoon ground cumin)
salt and pepper

Serves **4**
Prep time **20 minutes**

MEDITERRANEAN
Potato salad

4 Yellow Finn or white round
potatoes (about 1 lb), peeled
and cut into chunks
pinch of saffron threads
20 semi-dried tomatoes (about
4 oz), halved
¾ cup pitted black olives, coarsely
chopped
⅓ cup olive oil
¼ cup chia seeds
⅓ cup chopped basil leaves
3 tablespoons capers
salt and pepper

Serves **4**
Prep time **10 minutes,
plus cooling**
Cooking time **20 minutes**

1 Put the potatoes into a saucepan, pour in just enough cold water to cover them, and add the saffron. Bring to a boil, then cover and simmer gently for 15 minutes, until tender and cooked through. Drain and let cool.

2 Put the tomatoes, olives, oil, chia seeds, basil, and capers into a large bowl, add the cooled potatoes, and gently toss together. Season with a little salt and plenty of pepper.

3 Divide the salad between 4 serving bowls and serve with fresh crusty bread or a simple arugula salad, if liked.

VARIATION

For Mediterranean pasta salad, cook 8 oz dried pasta in a large saucepan of lightly salted boiling water for 8-10 minutes, until just tender. Drain well, rinse under cold water, and drain again. Put 20 semi-dried tomatoes (about 4 oz), coarsely chopped, ¾ cup coarsely chopped, pitted black olives, ⅓ cup of olive oil, ¼ cup of chia seeds, ⅓ cup chopped of basil leaves, and 3 tablespoons of capers into a large bowl. Combine with the pasta and toss well so that all the ingredients are well mixed. Season with salt and pepper before serving.

HERB-ROASTED
NEW POTATOES

1 Put the oil into a roasting pan and place in a preheated oven, at 400°F, for 5 minutes, until hot.

2 Add the potatoes, garlic, and herb sprigs, season well with salt and pepper, and turn to coat in the oil.

3 Return to the oven and roast for 40-45 minutes, turning occasionally, until the potatoes are crisp and tender. Serve hot.

VARIATION
For crushed new potatoes with scallions & mustard, cook 2 lb scrubbed new potatoes in a large saucepan of lightly salted, boiling water for 15 minutes or until tender. Drain well, return to the pan, and add 2 tablespoons of olive oil and 1 tablespoon whole-grain mustard. Crush with a fork until the potatoes are broken up but not mashed, then stir in 4 chopped scallions. Season to taste with salt and pepper and serve immediately.

2 tablespoons olive oil
2 lb new potatoes, scrubbed
4 garlic cloves, peeled but left whole
2 sprigs of rosemary
2 sprigs of thyme
1 sprig of sage
salt and pepper

Serves **6**
Prep time **10 minutes**
Cooking time **45-50 minutes**

AFFORDABILITY 1

NEW POTATO, BASIL & PINE NUT
SALAD

2 lb new potatoes, scrubbed
¼ cup extra virgin olive oil
1½ tablespoons vegan white
  wine vinegar
⅓ cup pine nuts
½ bunch of basil, leaves picked
salt and pepper

Serves **4-6**
Prep time **10 minutes,**
  plus cooling
Cooking time **15-18 minutes**

1   Cook the potatoes in a large saucepan of lightly salted boiling water for 12-15 minutes, until tender. Drain well and transfer to a large bowl. Cut any large potatoes in half.

2   Whisk together the oil, vinegar, and a little salt and pepper in a bowl. Add half to the potatoes, stir well, and let cool completely.

3   Toast the pine nuts in a dry skillet over medium heat, shaking the pan occasionally, for 2-3 minutes, until golden. Remove from the pan and let cool.

4   Mix the toasted pine nuts, remaining dressing, and basil with the potatoes, toss well, and then serve.

AFFORDABILITY
1

SPICY POTATO CURRY

1 Heat the oil in a large nonstick wok or skillet over medium-high heat. Add the mustard seeds, chili powder, cumin seeds, and curry leaves. Stir-fry for 1-2 minutes, until fragrant.

2 Add the ground spices and potatoes. Season to taste and stir-fry briskly over high heat for 4-5 minutes. Remove from the heat and stir in the cilantro. Squeeze the lemon juice over the top just before serving.

VARIATION
For quick curried spinach & potato sauté, follow the recipe above, then after the potatoes have been stir-fried for 4-5 minutes, gently fold in 3¹/₂ cups baby spinach. Stir-fry for 1-2 minutes, then remove from the heat, squeeze ¹/₄ cup of lemon juice over the top, and serve immediately with steamed rice or bread.

1 tablespoon peanut oil
1-2 teaspoons black mustard seeds
1 teaspoon chili powder or paprika
4 teaspoons cumin seeds
8-10 curry leaves
2 teaspoons ground cumin
2 teaspoons ground coriander
1 teaspoon ground turmeric
1 lb potatoes, peeled, boiled, and
    cut into 1 inc) cubes
¹/₃ cup chopped cilantro leaves
¹/₄ cup lemon juice
salt and pepper

Serves **4**
Prep time **20 minutes**
Cooking time **6-8 minutes**

AFFORDABILITY
1

ROASTED
VEGETABLES

1 small butternut squash
2 beets
1 potato
½ cassava
2 carrots
2 red onions
1 zucchini
½ cup avocado oil
1 tablespoon soy sauce
4 whole garlic cloves
2 teaspoons rosemary
2 teaspoons chopped fennel
   feathery top
salt and pepper

Serves **8**
Prep time **20 minutes**
Cooking time **45-50 minutes**

AFFORDABILITY

1 Preheat the oven to 350°F. Trim all the vegetables, then cut them into finger-size pieces.

2 Put the avocado oil and soy sauce into a large bowl and mix well. Dip all the vegetable pieces and garlic cloves in so that they are well coated.

3 Arrange the squash, beets, potato, and cassava in a baking pan and bake for 20 minutes.

4 Turn these vegetables over, then add the carrot, onions, zucchini, and garlic. Sprinkle with the rosemary and fennel, season with salt and pepper, then return the pan to the oven for another 25-30 minutes.

5 Serve with a variety of dips, such as hummus, Soynnaise (see page 218), or sweet chili sauce, and some warm bread.

SUMMER VEGETABLE
TEMPURA

1. Mix the dipping sauce ingredients together in a serving bowl and set aside.

2. Fill a deep saucepan halfway with vegetable oil and heat to 350–375°F, or until a cube of bread dropped into the oil browns in 30 seconds. Just before the oil is hot enough, using a handheld mixer, quickly beat the flour, cornstarch, salt, and sparkling water together in a bowl to make a slightly lumpy batter.

3. Dip one-third of the vegetables into the batter until coated, and then drop straight into the hot oil. Fry for 2 minutes, until crisp. Remove from the pan with a slotted spoon, drain on paper towels, and keep warm in a low oven.

4. Fry the remaining vegetables in another 2 batches. Serve hot with the dipping sauce.

vegetable oil, for deep-frying
2/3 cup all-purpose flour
2 tablespoons cornstarch
pinch of salt
1 cup ice-cold sparkling water
1 red bell pepper, cored, seeded, and cut into strips
12 thin asparagus spears, trimmed
1 zucchini, trimmed and sliced

Dipping sauce
2 tablespoons sweet chili sauce
2 tablespoons soy sauce
1 teaspoon finely grated lemon zest
1 tablespoon lemon juice

Serves **4**
Prep time **20 minutes**
Cooking time **15 minutes**

AFFORDABILITY
1

ITALIAN VEGETABLE
Kebabs

1 Put the chopped vegetables into a large bowl and toss in the olive oil, lemon juice, basil, and salt and pepper.

2 Thread the vegetables onto metal skewers and broil or put on the barbecue grill over medium heat for 10-12 minutes, turning occasionally, until cooked. Serve immediately.

2 red bell peppers, cored, seeded, and chopped
1 yellow bell pepper, cored, seeded, and chopped
2 zucchini, cut into thick slices
1 large red onion, cut into wedges
2 tablespoons olive oil
2 tablespoons lemon juice
2 tablespoons torn basil leaves
salt and pepper

Makes **4**
Prep time **10 minutes**
Cooking time **12 minutes**

STUDENT TIP

SHOP SEASONAL It's healthier and often cheaper to buy fruit and vegetables that are in season, and you also cut down on food miles. With farmers' markets becoming increasingly popular, you should find it easier to buy locally farmed produce on your doorstep.

AFFORDABILITY 1

EGGPLANT
WITH CAPER & MINT PESTO

1. Put the eggplant slices into a large bowl, pour the oil over them, and toss well, using both hands to coat as evenly as possible. The oil will be absorbed fast, so work as quickly as possible. Set aside for 10 minutes while you make the pesto.

2. Mix all the pesto ingredients together in a bowl. Season with a little salt and pepper.

3. Heat a ridged grill pan until smoking, then lay several of the eggplant slices onto the hot pan in a single layer and cook over high heat for 1-2 minutes on each side, until lightly charred and soft.

4. Transfer the eggplant to a heatproof platter and keep warm in a low oven while cooking the remaining slices.

5. Drizzle or spoon some of the pesto over the eggplant slices and serve with warm pita bread, with the remaining pesto on the side.

2 eggplants, trimmed and sliced
2/3 cup extra virgin olive oil
warm pita bread, to serve

Pesto
finely grated zest and juice of
   1 lemon
3 tablespoons olive oil
2 tablespoons vegan red
   wine vinegar
1/4 cup chopped mint, plus extra
   leaves to garnish
2 tablespoons capers, coarsely
   chopped
1 garlic clove, coarsely chopped
1 teaspoon sugar
salt and pepper

Serves **4**
Prep time **20 minutes**
Cooking time **15 minutes**

AFFORDABILITY 1

BROCCOLI
WITH GARLIC & CHILLI

5²/₃ cups broccoli florets
2 tablespoons peanut oil
2 garlic cloves, thinly sliced
2 teaspoons peeled and grated
  fresh ginger root
1-2 teaspoons dried chili flakes
salt and pepper

Serves **4**
Prep time **10 minutes**
Cooking time **5 minutes**

1 Cut the broccoli florets lengthwise into thin slices.

2 Bring a large saucepan of lightly salted water to a boil. Add the broccoli and blanch for 1-2 minutes. Drain and set aside.

3 Heat the oil in a large nonstick wok or skillet over high heat. Swirl the oil around, add the garlic, ginger, and chili flakes, and sizzle for 20-30 seconds, until fragrant.

4 Add the broccoli to the pan and stir-fry for 1-2 minutes, until just tender. Season with salt and pepper and serve immediately with cooked rice or noodles.

VARIATION

For cauliflower with garlic, chili & sesame, follow the recipe above, replacing the broccoli with 3 cups of cauliflower florets. When the dish is ready, sprinkle 2 tablespoons of toasted sesame seeds over the top and serve immediately.

AFFORDABILITY
1

Bok choy
WITH CHILI & GINGER

1 tablespoon peanut oil
½ chili, sliced into rings
1 tablespoon peeled and chopped
  fresh ginger root
large pinch of salt
1 lb bok choy, leaves separated
½ cup water
¼ teaspoon sesame oil

Serves **4**
Prep time **5 minutes**
Cooking time **5 minutes**

1 Heat the peanut oil in a wok or large skillet over high heat until the oil starts to shimmer. Add the chili, ginger, and salt and stir-fry for 15 seconds.

2 Add the bok choy to the pan and stir-fry for 1 minute, then add the measured water and continue cooking and stirring until the bok choy is tender and the water has evaporated.

3 Add the sesame oil to the pan, toss well, and serve immediately.

Spicy BEET & WALNUT PACKAGES

6 cooked beets
3 tablespoons olive oil
1 small red onion, chopped
2 celery stalks, chopped
2 teaspoons cumin seeds
2/3 cup broken walnuts
2/3 cup vegan mayonnaise or
  Soynnaise (see page 218)
2 teaspoons harissa or chipotle
  paste
4 sheets of phyllo pastry
salt and pepper
greens, to serve

Serves **3-4**
Prep time **25 minutes**
Cooking time **30 minutes**

1 Preheat the oven to 400°F. Coarsely grate the beets into a bowl.

2 Heat 1 tablespoon of the oil in a skillet and sauté the onion and celery for 3 minutes to soften. Add to the beets, along with the cumin seeds, walnuts, and a little salt and pepper. Mix well.

3 Beat together the mayonnaise and harissa or chipotle paste and transfer to a small serving dish.

4 Lay one sheet of phyllo pastry on the work surface and brush with a little of the remaining oil. Lay a second sheet of pastry on top. Cut into six squares.

5 Spoon a little of the beet mixture onto the center of each square so you use about half the filling altogether, spreading the mixture toward the edges. Fold 2 opposite sides of one square over the filling, then roll up from an unfolded edge to make a package. Place on a baking sheet. Repeat with the remaining 5 squares, then use the remaining phyllo sheets and filling to make another 6 packages. Brush with the remaining oil.

6 Bake for 20-25 minutes, until crisp and golden. Serve with the spicy mayonnaise and greens.

SPINACH DAHL
with
CHERRY TOMATOES

1 Put the lentils into a strainer and rinse under cold running water until the water runs clear. Drain and transfer to a wide saucepan with the coconut milk, broth, cumin, coriander, turmeric, and ginger.

2 Bring the mixture to a boil, skimming off any scum as it rises to the surface, and then cover. Reduce the heat and simmer for 15-20 minutes, stirring occasionally to prevent the mixture from sticking to the bottom of the saucepan. Stir in the spinach and cherry tomatoes and cook for 6-8 minutes or until the lentils are soft and tender, adding a little broth or water if the mixture seems too thick.

3 Meanwhile, make the "tarka." Heat the oil in a small skillet and sauté the shallots, garlic, ginger, chili powder, and cumin and mustard seeds, stirring often. Cook for 3-4 minutes, until the shallots are lightly browned, and then combine this mixture into the cooked lentils.

4 Stir in the garam masala and chopped cilantro, then check the seasoning. Serve with naan or rice.

AFFORDABILITY
1

1½ cups red split lentils
1 cup coconut milk
2½ cups vegetable broth (see page 219)
1 teaspoon ground cumin
1 teaspoon ground coriander
1 teaspoon ground turmeric
1 teaspoon ground ginger
1 (10 oz) package spinach, chopped
16 cherry tomatoes
¼ teaspoon garam masala
⅔ cup finely chopped cilantro (leaves and stems)
salt and pepper

Tarka
2 tablespoons sunflower oil
4 shallots, thinly sliced
3 garlic cloves, thinly sliced
1 teaspoon finely chopped fresh ginger root
¼ teaspoon chili powder
2 teaspoons cumin seeds
1 teaspoon black mustard seeds

Serves **4**
Prep time **5 minutes**
Cooking time **30 minutes**

ZUCCHINI & EGGPLANT
FAJITAS

4-5 zucchini (about 1½ lb), cut into chip-size pieces

2 medium eggplants (about 1 lb), cut into french fry-size pieces

2 red onions, sliced

¼ cup mild olive oil or vegetable oil

2 teaspoons ground cumin

2 ripe avocados

1 garlic clove, crushed

1 teaspoon lime juice

⅔ cup coconut cream, chilled (not sweetened creamed coconut)

16 cherry tomatoes, chopped

2 scallions, finely chopped

1 red chili, seeded and finely chopped

3 tablespoons chopped cilantro

8 plain, whole-wheat or seeded wraps

1 cup shredded cheddar-style vegan cheese

salt and pepper

Makes **8**
Prep time **40 minutes**
Cooking time **1¼ - 1½ hours**

1 Preheat the oven to 400°F. Put the zucchini, eggplants, and onions into a roasting pan. Drizzle with the oil and sprinkle with the cumin and a little salt and pepper. Toss the ingredients together and bake for 1¼ -1½ hours, turning the vegetables several times during cooking.

2 Mash the avocado in a bowl and beat in the garlic, lime juice, and plenty of freshly ground black pepper. In a separate bowl, whip the coconut cream using a handheld mixer or wire balloon whisk until softly peaking.

3 Combine the tomatoes with the scallions, chili, and cilantro and set aside. Seal the wraps in a sheet of aluminum foil and place on an oven shelf below the roasting vegetables. Heat through for 10 minutes.

4 To serve, spoon the vegetables down the centers of the wraps, top with the tomato salsa, coconut cream, mashed avocado, and Cheddar-style vegan cheese. Wrap and serve.

AFFORDABILITY
1

BAG SHARING
pizza

AFFORDABILITY 1

1. Put the flour, salt, sugar, yeast, and 2 tablespoons of the oil in a bowl. Add the measured water and mix with a blunt knife to make a soft dough.

2. Turn out onto a floured surface and knead for 10 minutes, until the dough is smooth and elastic.

3. Put into a large, lightly oiled bowl, cover with plastic wrap, and let rise in a warm place for 30-40 minutes, until risen to twice the size.

4. While proving, heat another 2 tablespoons of the oil in a skillet and cook the fennel for 6-8 minutes, until golden. Push to one side of the pan, add the fennel seeds, if using, and the asparagus, and cook for another 2 minutes.

5. Turn out the dough onto a floured surface and roll out to a rectangle measuring about 15 x 12½ inches, or the size of your largest baking sheet. Place the dough on the baking sheet and spread the vegan pesto over the pizza, leaving the edges clear. Sprinkle the fennel and asparagus over the pizza along with the artichokes and peas. Bake for 18-20 minutes in a preheated oven, at 475°F, until the dough is risen and golden.

6. Drizzle with the remaining oil and a squeeze of lemon or lime juice. Sprinkle with basil leaves and serve, cut into squares.

2 cups white bread flour, plus extra for dusting
1 teaspoon salt
1 teaspoon sugar
2 teaspoons active dry yeast
⅓ cup olive oil
1 cup lukewarm water
1 large fennel bulb, thinly sliced
1 teaspoon fennel seeds (optional)
12 asparagus spears, trimmed and halved lengthwise
⅓ cup vegan pesto (with tofu)
7 artichoke hearts (from a jar), drained
⅔ cup fresh or frozen peas
squeeze of lemon or lime juice
fresh basil leaves, to garnish

Serves **4-5**
Prep time **30 minutes, plus proving**
Cooking time **30 minutes**

CABBAGE PATTIES

AFFORDABILITY 1

1 Mix the potato, red cabbage, onion, flour, baking powder, soy milk, and Dijon mustard together in a large bowl, season with salt and pepper, and form into 4 patties.

2 Heat the coconut oil in a nonstick skillet, then cook the patties over medium heat until golden brown on both sides.

3 Serve with hot baked beans, broiled tomatoes, and mushrooms or scrambled tofu.

2 tablespoons mashed or baked potato
2 tablespoons finely chopped red cabbage
1 small onion, chopped
2 tablespoons whole-wheat flour
pinch of baking powder
1 tablespoon soy milk
1 teaspoon vegan Dijon mustard
salt and pepper
1 tablespoon coconut oil, for frying

Serves **2**
Prep time **5 minutes**
Cooking time **5 minutes**

STUDENT TIP

SEPARATE UTENSILS If you don't like using pans, knives, and cutting boards that have been in contact with meat, keep a separate set of clearly marked kitchen equipment for your own use. If you have a lot of housemates, a plastic container in your room might be the best option.

SMOKY TOFU
& POTATO HASH

1 Cook the potatoes in boiling, lightly salted water for
10 minutes, until tender. Drain thoroughly.

2 Drain the tofu of any liquid and squeeze between layers of
paper towels until you've removed as much of the moisture
as you can. Sprinkle the paprika, bouillon powder ,and flour
on a plate. Tear the tofu into pieces and add to the plate.
Lightly dust with the flour mixture.

3 Combine the ketchup, tomato paste, and measured water
in a bowl.

4 Heat 1 tablespoon of the oil in a skillet and sauté the
leek and onion for 5 minutes, stirring until softened. Add
the remaining oil, tofu, and potatoes and cook for another
2-3 minutes. Add the tomato liquid, cherry tomatoes, and
spinach and heat through for a couple of minutes, stirring
until the spinach has wilted. Serve immediately.

2 medium baking potatoes, cut
into small chunks
7 oz tofu
1/2 teaspoon smoked paprika
1/2 teaspoon vegan bouillon
powder
1 teaspoon all-purpose flour
2 tablespoons ketchup
1 tablespoon tomato paste
1/2 cup water
2 tablespoons vegetable oil
1 small leek, thinly sliced
1 onion, thinly sliced
8-10 cherry tomatoes, halved
3 1/2 cups baby spinach

Serves **2**
Prep time **10 minutes**
Cooking time **20 minutes**

TOMATO & MUSHROOM
RAGOUT
on sourdough

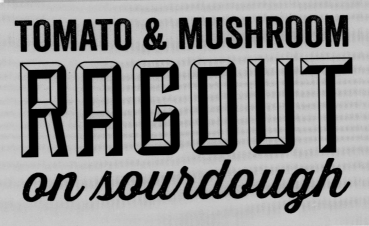

1 Heat 1 tablespoon of the oil in a skillet and sauté the onion for 3 minutes, until softened. Add the mushrooms and sauté for about 5 minutes, until the juices have evaporated and the mushrooms begin to brown.

2 Stir in the sun-dried tomatoes, cherry tomatoes, and half the basil, and season with salt and pepper.

3 Toast the bread slices, rub with the cut sides of the garlic, and place on serving plates.

4 Drizzle with the remaining oil and spoon the sauce on top. Serve sprinkled with the remaining basil.

2 tablespoons olive oil
1 red onion, chopped
3¼ cups coarsely chopped cremini mushrooms
⅓ cup drained and chopped sun-dried tomatoes in oil
8 cherry tomatoes, quartered
½ cup coarsely torn basil leaves
2 slices of sourdough bread
1 garlic clove, halved
salt and pepper

Serves **2**
Prep time **10 minutes**
Cooking time **10 minutes**

AFFORDABILITY
1

FLASH-IN-THE-PAN
RATATOUILLE

1 Heat the oil in a large skillet until hot and stir-fry all of the vegetables, except the diced tomatoes, for a few minutes. Add the tomatoes, balsamic vinegar, and sugar, season, and stir well. Cover tightly and simmer for 15 minutes, until the vegetables are cooked.

2 Remove from the heat, sprinkle with the olives and torn basil, and serve.

½ cup olive oil
2 onions, chopped
1 eggplant, cut into ¾ inch cubes
2 large zucchini, cut into ¾ inch cubes
1 red bell pepper, cored, seeded and cut into ¾ inch pieces
1 yellow pepper, cored, seeded, and cut into ¾ inch pieces
2 garlic cloves, crushed
1 (14½ oz) can diced tomatoes
2–3 tablespoons balsamic vinegar
1 teaspoon packed brown sugar
10–12 black olives, pitted
salt and pepper
torn basil leaves, to garnish

Serves **4**
Prep time **10 minutes**
Cooking time **20 minutes**

AFFORDABILITY
1

CURRIED
CABBAGE
& CARROT
Stir-fry

1 tablespoon peanut oil
4 shallots, finely chopped
2 teaspoons peeled and finely
    grated fresh ginger root
2 teaspoons finely grated garlic
2 fresh long green chilies, halved
    lengthwise
2 teaspoons cumin seeds
1 teaspoon ground turmeric
1 teaspoon coriander seeds,
    crushed
1 large carrot, coarsely grated
3 cups shredded green cabbage
1 tablespoon curry powder
salt and pepper

Serves **4**
Prep time **10 minutes**
Cooking time **about 15 minutes**

1 Heat the oil in a large nonstick wok or skillet over low heat.
   Add the shallots, ginger, garlic, and chilies and stir-fry for
   2–3 minutes, until the shallots have softened. Add the cumin
   seeds, turmeric, and crushed coriander seeds and stir-fry
   for 1 minute.

2 Increase the heat to high and add the carrot and cabbage,
   tossing well to coat in the spice mixture. Add the curry
   powder and season to taste.

3 Cover the pan and cook over medium-low heat for
   10 minutes, stirring occasionally.

4 Remove from the heat and serve immediately with
   steamed rice.

AFFORDABILITY
1

STIR-FRIED VEGETABLE RICE

1. Heat the oil in a large, nonstick wok and add the scallions, garlic, and ginger. Stir-fry for 4–5 minutes, then add the red bell pepper, carrot, and peas. Stir-fry over high heat for 3–4 minutes.

2. Stir in the rice, soy sauce, and sweet chili sauce and stir-fry for 3–4 minutes or until the rice is heated through and piping hot.

3. Remove from the heat and serve immediately, garnished with the chopped herbs.

2 tablespoons sunflower oil
6 scallions, cut diagonally into 1 inch lengths
2 garlic cloves, crushed
1 teaspoon finely grated fresh ginger root
1 red bell pepper, cored, seeded, and finely chopped
1 carrot, peeled and finely diced
2 cups peas
4 cups cooked, white long-grain rice
1 tablespoon dark soy sauce
1 tablespoon sweet chili sauce

To garnish
cilantro, coarsely chopped
mint, coarsely chopped

Serves **4**
Prep time **10 minutes**
Cooking time **15 minutes**

AFFORDABILITY 1

CARROT & PEA PILAF

1½ cups basmati rice or other
   long-grain rice
¼ cup sunflower oil
1 cinnamon stick
2 teaspoons cumin seeds
2 cloves
4 cardamom pods, lightly bruised
8 black peppercorns
1 large carrot, peeled and
   shredded
1⅓ cups frozen peas
2 cups hot water
salt and pepper

....
Serves **4**
Prep time **20 minutes,**
   plus soaking and standing
Cooking time **about 15 minutes**
....

1 Wash the rice several times in cold water, then let soak for 15 minutes. Drain thoroughly.

2 Heat the oil in a heavy saucepan and add the spices. Stir-fry for 2–3 minutes, then add the carrot and peas. Stir-fry for another 2–3 minutes, then add the rice. Stir and pour in the measured hot water. Season well.

3 Bring to a boil, cover tightly, reduce the heat, and simmer gently for 10 minutes. Do not lift the lid, because the steam is necessary for the cooking process.

4 Remove the pan from the heat and let the rice stand, covered and undisturbed, for 8–10 minutes. Fluff up the grains with a fork and serve immediately.

AFFORDABILITY **2**

Asian-style RISOTTO

AFFORDABILITY
2

1 Bring the broth, soy sauce, and mirin to a simmer in a saucepan. Meanwhile, heat 2 tablespoons of the sunflower oil and the sesame oil in a separate saucepan, add the scallions, garlic, and ginger, and cook over high heat, stirring, for 1 minute. Stir in the rice and lime leaves and cook over low heat for 1 minute, until glossy.

2 Stir ⅔ cup of the broth mixture into the rice and simmer, stirring, until it is almost all absorbed. Add the broth, a little at a time, and simmer, stirring, until all but a ladleful has been absorbed. Meanwhile, slice all but a few of the mushrooms. Heat the remaining oil in a skillet, add the mushrooms, and cook over medium heat, stirring frequently, for 5 minutes, until golden.

3 Add the cilantro to the risotto with the sliced mushrooms and the remaining broth. Simmer, stirring frequently, until almost all the broth is absorbed and the rice is tender and cooked through. Serve garnished with the whole mushrooms and cilantro sprigs.

5 cups vegetable broth
  (see page 219)
1 tablespoon dark soy sauce
2 tablespoons mirin
3 tablespoons sunflower oil
1 tablespoon sesame oil
bunch of scallions, thickly sliced
2 garlic cloves, chopped
1 inch piece of fresh ginger root,
  peeled and grated
2 cups risotto rice
6 kaffir lime leaves
8 oz shiitake mushrooms, wiped
  clean and stems discarded
⅓ cup chopped cilantro, plus extra
  sprigs to garnish

Serves **4**
Preparation time **15 minutes**
Cooking time **25 minutes**

STUDENT TIP

BUY IN BULK Dry goods, cans, and multipacks are all good items to buy when on sale, because they'll keep for ages. Find an extra cupboard or clear some space under your bed to store your extra groceries.

GINGER, COCONUT & LIME LEAF *Rice*

1⅓ cups jasmine rice
2 teaspoons chopped fresh
  ginger root
1¼ cups coconut milk
6 kaffir lime leaves, bashed
1 lemongrass stalk, halved and
  bruised
1 teaspoon salt
1 cup water

Serves **4**
Prep time **10 minutes,**
  plus standing
Cooking time **15 minutes**

1 Put the rice into a strainer and rinse in cold water until the water runs clear. Drain and shake well.

2 Combine the rice with all the remaining ingredients in a saucepan with a tight-fitting lid. Bring to a boil, cover with the lid, and cook over low heat for 10 minutes.

3 Remove from the heat and let stand, covered and without stirring, for 10 minutes. Fluff up with a fork before serving.

VARIATION
For cardamom & lemon rice, rinse and drain 1⅓ cups basmati rice or other long-grain rice as above. Heat 1 tablespoon of sunflower oil in a large saucepan with a tight-fitting lid, add 1 chopped onion, and cook gently for 2–3 minutes, until softened. Stir in 6 crushed cardamom pods and the rice and stir-fry for 2–3 minutes, then pour in 2 cups boiling water. Season with salt and stir well, cover with the lid, and cook over low heat for 10 minutes. Remove from the heat and stir in the juice of 2 lemons. Let stand, covered and without stirring, for 10 minutes. Fluff up with a fork before serving.

SPICY RICE
with Lentils

1 Wash the lentils and rice several times in cold water. Drain thoroughly.

2 Heat the oil in a heavy saucepan and add the onion. Stir-fry for 6-8 minutes over medium heat, then add the spices.

3 Continue to stir-fry for 2-3 minutes, then add the rice and lentils. Stir-fry for another 2-3 minutes, then add the broth, tomatoes, and fresh cilantro. Season well and bring to a boil. Reduce the heat, cover tightly, and simmer for 10 minutes.

4 Remove the pan from the heat and let stand undisturbed for 10 minutes. Transfer to a serving dish and garnish with crispy fried onions.

5 Serve immediately with pickled vegetables and plain soy yogurt, if liked.

$2/3$ cup red split lentils
$1\frac{1}{4}$ cups basmati rice or other long-grain rice
3 tablespoons sunflower oil
1 onion, finely chopped
1 teaspoon ground turmeric
1 tablespoon cumin seeds
1 dried red chili
1 cinnamon stick
3 cloves
3 cardamom pods, lightly bruised
2 cups vegetable broth (see page 219)
8 cherry tomatoes, halved
$1/3$ cup finely chopped cilantro leaves
salt and pepper
crispy fried onions, to garnish

Serves **4**
Prep time **20 minutes, plus standing**
Cooking time **20-25 minutes**

BOOSTER
SNACKS

It's not always possible to plan for three healthy meals every day. Deadlines, empty cupboards, and late nights are common reasons for coming home and slumping on the couch with a couple of pieces of toast instead of a nutritious stir-fry or salad. However, there's a wide selection of natural snacks that you can nibble on during the day to give you an energy boost and bolster your vitamin intake, so that the odd days of unhealthy meals won't take the edge off your energy levels.

Buy dried ingredients in bulk for better value, and split them into handy servings that you can throw into your bag before you leave the house.

NUTS

Nutritious, healthy, and long-lasting, nuts are the ultimate vegan snack. Just a handful will give you an instant energy boost and keep you going until your next meal. Cashew nuts are particularly beneficial for vegans, because they're high in zinc and iron, while pistachios contain valuable antioxidants and a high level of potassium.

BLUEBERRIES
Packed full of vitamins, fiber, and antioxidants, these little berries are the perfect midmorning snack. You can also sprinkle a handful over cereal or oatmeal, or keep them in the freezer and use for smoothies.

SEEDS
By buying a few essential seeds, such as pumpkin, sunflower, and chia, you can make your own seed mix to nibble on between classes. You can also sprinkle them over salads, add them to oat bars, cakes, and granola bars, and toast or grind them for bulking up main meals.

SEAWEED
Full of iodine, crispy seaweed makes a great nutritious snack. You can buy different varieties of seaweed in Asian grocery stores and supermarkets, but always check the packaging to make sure it's a vegan product; some of the seasonings may contain nonvegan ingredients.

POPCORN
If you want a crispy snack, reach for the popcorn instead of potato chips. However, store-bought popcorn have added salt and flavorings that outweigh the nutritional benefits. Fortunately, it's easy to make it yourself (and much cheaper)—and you'll be getting higher levels of protein and fiber, and you will know exactly what you're adding in terms of flavor. A little salt mixed with a pinch of dried chili flakes is a good combination.

Hot & Smoky
HUMMUS

1 (15 oz) can chickpeas (garbanzo
  beans), drained and rinsed
3 tablespoons lemon juice
1 large garlic clove, crushed
2 tablespoons light tahini
1 tablespoon hot smoked paprika,
  plus extra for sprinkling
1/2 teaspoon ground cumin
2/3 cup extra virgin olive oil, plus
  extra for drizzling
2 tablespoons sesame seeds
salt and pepper

To serve
4 pieces of Lebanese or Turkish
  flatbread
crunchy raw vegetables (optional)

Serves **4**
Prep time **12 minutes**
Cooking time **20 minutes**

1 Put all the ingredients, except the olive oil and sesame seeds, into a food processor and blend until smooth. With the machine still running, slowly drizzle the olive oil into the chickpea paste until it is completely incorporated. Season with salt and pepper and scrape into a small dish.

2 Heat a dry, nonstick skillet and toast the sesame seeds over moderately low heat, moving them quickly around the pan until they are golden brown.

3 Stir most of the sesame seeds into the hummus and sprinkle the rest over the top.

4 Wrap the flatbread in aluminum foil and heat in a preheated oven, at 325°F, for 20 minutes, until warmed through.

5 Drizzle the hummus with olive oil, sprinkle with paprika, and serve with the warm flatbread and crunchy vegetables, if you want.

RED PEPPER & EGGPLANT
HUMMUS

1   Preheat the oven to 375°F. Arrange the red bell pepper, garlic cloves, and eggplant in a single layer in a large roasting pan. Drizzle with the chili oil, sprinkle with the fennel seeds, if using, and season with salt and pepper. Roast for 35–40 minutes or until softened and golden. Let the vegetables cool, but do not turn off the oven.

2   Squeeze the soft garlic out of its skin and put into a food processor or blender with the roasted vegetables, three-quarters of the chickpeas, and the tahini. Blend until almost smooth, season with salt and pepper, then spoon into a serving bowl. Let cool and cover.

3   Cut the pita breads into 1 inch strips and put into a large bowl. Spray with a little olive oil and toss with the paprika and a little salt until well coated. Spread out in a single layer on a baking sheet. Toast in the oven for 10–12 minutes or until crisp.

4   Sprinkle the hummus with the remaining chickpeas and toasted sesame seeds and drizzle with 1–2 tablespoons chili oil. Serve with the toasted pita breads.

1 red bell pepper, cored, seeded, and quartered
3 garlic cloves, unpeeled and lightly crushed
1 eggplant, trimmed and cut into large chunks
1 tablespoon chili oil, plus extra to serve
1½ teaspoons fennel seeds (optional)
1 (15 oz) can chickpeas (garbanzo beans), drained and rinsed
1 tablespoon tahini
1 teaspoon sesame seeds, lightly toasted
salt and pepper

To serve
4 whole-wheat pita breads
olive oil spray
1 teaspoon paprika
salt

Serves **4-6**
Prep time **10 minutes, plus cooling**
Cooking time **50 minutes**

FENNEL, APPLE & RED CABBAGE *Slaw*

¼ red cabbage, shredded
1 fennel bulb, trimmed and thinly
    sliced
1 sweet, crisp apple, such as Pink
    Lady, cored and thinly sliced
1 small red onion, thinly sliced
1 celery stalk, sliced
2 tablespoons sunflower seeds
2 tablespoons pumpkin seeds
⅓ cup vegan mayonnaise or
    Soynnaise (see page 218)
1 tablespoon lemon juice
1 teaspoon vegan Dijon mustard
small handful of flat leaf parsley,
    coarsely chopped
salt and pepper

Serves **4**
Prep time **20 minutes**

1 Put the cabbage into a large bowl, add the fennel, apple, onion, celery, and sunflower and pumpkin seeds, and toss well to combine.

2 Mix the mayonnaise, lemon juice, and mustard together in a small bowl and season with salt and pepper.

3 Add to the cabbage mixture along with the parsley and gently toss together to coat all the ingredients in the dressing.

STUDENT TIP

PAY BY CASH Bringing cash instead of cards to the supermarket can help you stick to your budget. You'll have to buy within your means, shop wisely, and add up your purchases as you go. And, if you do manage to find a few bargains, you can spend the extra on a treat or two.

SEEDED FRIES
WITH RED PEPPER DIP

3 sweet potatoes (about 1 lb),
  peeled and cut into wedges
4 white round potatoes (about
  1 lb), peeled and cut into wedges
¼ cup olive oil
1 tablespoon poppy seeds
1 tablespoon sesame seeds
1 teaspoon dried chili flakes
1 large red bell pepper, cored,
  seeded, and cut into 4 wedges
2 tomatoes, halved
½ teaspoon smoked paprika
3 tablespoons chopped cilantro
salt and pepper

Serves **4**
Prep time **20 minutes**
Cooking time **35 minutes**

1 Preheat the oven to 400°F. Drizzle the sweet potato and white potato wedges with 3 tablespoons of the olive oil in a large roasting pan and toss well, then sprinkle with the poppy and sesame seeds and chili flakes and toss again.

2 Season generously with salt and pepper and roast in the top of the oven for 35 minutes, until golden.

3 Meanwhile, put the red pepper wedges and tomatoes into a smaller roasting pan, then drizzle with the remaining olive oil and toss well. Roast on a lower shelf in the oven for 25 minutes, until softened and lightly charred in places. Let cool.

4 Transfer the roasted red pepper and tomatoes to a food processor, season generously with salt and pepper, and add the smoked paprika. Process until almost smooth but with a little texture still remaining.

5 Spoon into a small serving bowl and place in the center of a serving platter. Arrange the roasted potato wedges on the platter, sprinkle with the chopped cilantro, and serve.

AFFORDABILITY
1

EGGPLANT DIP
& crispy tortillas

1 Preheat the oven to 425°F. Put the eggplant in a bowl with ⅓ cup of the extra virgin olive oil and toss well.

2 Transfer to a large roasting pan and roast for 25 minutes, until soft and lightly charred in places. Let cool.

3 Transfer the eggplant to a food processor and add the garlic, ¼ teaspoon of the smoked paprika, the tahini, lemon juice, half the chopped parsley, and plenty of salt and pepper. Process until smooth, then transfer to a serving bowl.

4 Mix the remaining extra virgin olive oil with the remaining paprika and use it to swirl over the top of the dip. Sprinkle with the remaining chopped parsley.

5 Brush each tortilla triangle lightly with the olive oil and spread them evenly across 1 or 2 large baking sheets. Sprinkle with the salt and cook them under a preheated medium broiler for 1-2 minutes, until lightly crisp and golden. Arrange the tortillas around the dip bowl and serve.

1 large eggplant (about 1½ lb), trimmed and cut into thick chunks
½ cup extra virgin olive oil
1 garlic clove, crushed
½ teaspoon smoked paprika
3 tablespoons tahini
juice of 1 lemon
1 tablespoon chopped flat leaf parsley
salt and pepper

Tortillas
6 mini flour tortillas, cut into triangles
1 tablespoon olive oil
1 teaspoon sea salt flakes

Serves **6**
Prep time **15 minutes,** plus cooling
Cooking time **30 minutes**

AFFORDABILITY

THE MAIN EVENT

POTATO, ROSEMARY
& ONION POT PIE

QUICK VEGETABLE MOLE

TAGLIATELLE WITH SQUASH
& SAGE

SPICED ONION PANCAKES
WITH RED LENTILS & CHICKPEAS

3 tablespoons vegetable oil,
  plus extra for shallow-frying
4 garlic cloves, crushed
2 tablespoons curry leaves
3 large onions, thinly sliced
3 carrots, cut into small dice
1 cup red lentils, rinsed
¼ cup finely chopped fresh
  ginger root
1 teaspoon ground turmeric
2 teaspoons ground cumin
1 red chili, seeded and finely
  chopped
4 cups vegetable broth
  (see page 219)
1 (15 oz) can chickpeas
  (garbanzo beans)
⅓ cup all-purpose flour
¼ cup chopped cilantro
salt and pepper

Serves **4**
Prep time **25 minutes**
Cooking time **45 minutes**

1 Heat the 3 tablespoons of oil in a large, shallow saucepan and sauté the garlic and curry leaves for 30 seconds. Lift out with a slotted spoon onto a plate.

2 To make the lentils, transfer one-third of the sliced onions into the oil and sauté gently for 5 minutes. Add the carrots, red lentils, ginger, turmeric, cumin, chili, and broth. Bring to a simmer and cover with a lid. Cook gently for 30 minutes, until the lentils are tender and turning mushy.

3 Drain the chickpeas, reserving the liquid. Measure ½ cup of the chickpea liquid, pour into a bowl, and whisk using a handheld electric mixer or wire balloon whisk until foamy. Sprinkle in the flour and stir in to make a paste. Add the remaining onions, cilantro, and a little salt and pepper and mix well.

4 Stir the chickpeas, curry leaves, and garlic into the lentils and heat through gently while preparing the onion pancakes, adding a dash of hot water if the lentils become too thick.

5 Pour a thin film of oil into a skillet and heat. Add spoonfuls of the onion mixture and flatten down gently. Cook for about 2 minutes, until golden on the underside. Flip over and cook for another 1–2 minutes. Drain on paper towels while you cook any remaining onion batter. Serve with the lentils and chickpeas.

RICE CREPES
with veggie chowder

1. Mix the rice flour, fennel seeds, all-purpose flour, salt, and measured cold water to make the rice crepe batter. Let stand for about 2 hours.

2. For the chowder, heat the oil in a large saucepan and gently sauté the onions, fennel, and carrots for 10 minutes. Add the garlic and sauté for another 2 minutes. Stir in the tomatoes, curry paste, broth, tomato paste, and turmeric and bring to a simmer. Cover with a lid and cook gently for 20 minutes.

3. Add the green beans and peas, cover, and cook for another 10 minutes, until the vegetables are completely tender.

4. Meanwhile, cook the crepes. Heat a little oil in a small skillet or crepe pan until just smoking. Give the batter a stir and pour a small ladleful into the pan, spreading it slightly with the bottom of the ladle. Cook until set and pale golden on the underside. Turn and briefly cook the other side.

5. Transfer to a plate and keep warm while cooking the remaining batter in the same way, oiling the pan again when necessary. If the pan is large enough, you'll be able to cook 2 or 3 at the same time.

6. Transfer the chowder to serving bowls, sprinkle with the cilantro, and serve with the warm crepes.

1²/₃ cups rice flour
2 teaspoons fennel seeds
3 tablespoons all-purpose flour
1½ teaspoons salt
1²/₃ cups cold water
vegetable oil, for frying

Chowder

2 tablespoons vegetable oil
2 large onions, chopped
1 fennel bulb, coarsely chopped
3 carrots, coarsely chopped
4 garlic cloves, chopped
¾ cup canned diced tomatoes
2–3 tablespoons vegan mild curry paste
2 cups vegetable broth (see page 219)
2 tablespoons tomato paste
1 teaspoon ground turmeric
2 cups trimmed and thinly sliced green beans
²/₃ cup fresh or frozen peas
⅓ cup chopped cilantro

Serves **4**
Prep time **30 minutes, plus standing**
Cooking time **50 minutes**

AFFORDABILITY
1

ZUCCHINI
STUFFED WITH WALNUT AND LENTIL PÂTÉ

4 zucchini
1 tablespoon avocado or olive oil
1 tablespoon soy sauce

Pâté
2/3 cup red lentils
1/2 onion, chopped
1 garlic clove, chopped
1 cup vegetable broth
  (see page 219)
1/4 cup chopped walnuts
1 teaspoon apple cider vinegar
1 teaspoon yeast extract
2 teaspoons chopped dates
1 tablespoon canola oil
1 teaspoon soy milk
1 teaspoon chopped thyme

Serves **4**
Prep time **15 minutes**
Cooking time **45-50 minutes**

1 First make the pâté. Fill a medium saucepan with cold water, add the lentils, and bring to a boil.

2 Drain the lentils, rinse under running cold water, then return them to the saucepan. Add the onion, garlic, and vegetable broth and bring to a boil, then simmer for 20 minutes.

3 Drain the lentils again, then stir in all the remaining pâté ingredients. Transfer the mixture to a food processor or liquidizer and blend until smooth.

4 Slice a thin sliver from the bottom of the zucchini so that they sit level on a plate. Cut a rectangle almost the length and width of the zucchini through the skin on the top side. Carefully remove the rectangle of skin, then scoop out the flesh using a teaspoon. (Freeze the flesh to use later in another recipe.)

5 Mix together the avocado or olive oil and soy sauce, then brush the cut surfaces of the zucchini with it. Bake for about 15 minutes in a preheated oven, at 350°F. Remove the zucchini from the oven, fill with the lentil pâté, and return to the oven for 5-10 minutes to heat through.

6 Serve with a mixed salad, chutney or other fruity condiment, and warm oat cakes.

Stuffed MUSHROOMS

2 large portobello mushrooms
2 tablespoons olive oil, plus extra
  for oiling
2 scallions, chopped
½ red bell pepper, cored, seeded,
  and chopped
1 small zucchini, chopped
4 olives, pitted and chopped
2 tablespoons rolled oats
1 tablespoon chopped basil
1 tablespoon soy sauce
1 tablespoon lime juice
salt and pepper
mixed greens, to serve

Serves **2**
Prep time **5 minutes**
Cooking time **20-25 minutes**

1 Preheat the oven to 350°F. Remove the mushroom stems and chop them.

2 Heat the oil in a small saucepan and gently sauté the mushroom stems, scallions, red bell pepper, zucchini, olives, and oats until the oats are golden. Stir in the basil, soy sauce, and lime juice.

3 Oil the mushroom caps and put them onto a baking sheet. Spoon the oat mixture onto the mushrooms, season with salt and pepper, and bake for 15-20 minutes, until the caps start to soften.

4 Serve the hot mushrooms immediately on a bed of mixed greens.

AFFORDABILITY
1

Turkish Stuffed BUTTERNUT SQUASH

1 Sit the squash halves, cut side up, in a large roasting pan, brush each with 1 tablespoon of oil, and season with salt and pepper. Roast in a preheated oven, at 425°F), for 45 minutes, until lightly charred on top.

2 Meanwhile, heat the oil for the filling in a large, heavy skillet, add the onion, garlic, and cumin, and cook over medium-high heat, stirring occasionally, for 4-5 minutes, until beginning to soften. Add the tomatoes, parsley, oregano, and tomato paste and cook, stirring occasionally, for another 5 minutes. Season well with salt and pepper.

3 Divide the filling among the cavities of the roasted squash halves and sprinkle with the cumin seeds. Reduce the oven temperature to 350°F, and roast the stuffed squash for 20 minutes or until the filling is soft and golden in places. Serve with a simple salad of peppery greens, if you want.

2 butternut squash, halved and seeded
¼ cup olive oil
salt and pepper

Filling
3 tablespoons olive oil
1 large onion, finely chopped
1 garlic clove, thinly sliced
1 teaspoon ground cumin
4 tomatoes (about 1 lb), coarsely chopped
¼ cup chopped flat leaf parsley
1 tablespoon chopped oregano
2 tablespoons tomato paste
1 teaspoon cumin seeds
salt and pepper

Serves **4**
Prep time **25 minutes**
Cooking time **1 hour 5 minutes**

AFFORDABILITY

QUINOA-STUFFED TOMATOES

¼ cup quinoa, rinsed and drained
4 large beefsteak tomatoes
½ small red onion, finely chopped
⅓ cup drained and sliced roasted
   red peppers from a jar
1 red chili, seeded and chopped
2 tablespoons chopped
   flat leaf parsley
2 tablespoon chopped cilantro
2 tablespoons sunflower seeds
1 teaspoon sesame oil
1 tablespoon soy sauce, plus extra
   to serve
2 tablespoons olive oil
pepper

Serves **4**
Prep time **20 minutes**
Cooking time **40-50 minutes**

1 Add the quinoa to a saucepan of boiling water, then simmer for 10-12 minutes, until tender. Drain, rinse in cold water, and drain again.

2 Meanwhile, cut the tops off the tomatoes and hollow out the centers with a teaspoon. Put half the tomato pulp and seeds into a bowl, discarding the rest, and add the onion, roasted red peppers, chili, parsley, cilantro, and sunflower seeds, and mix well.

3 Stir the sesame oil and soy sauce together and pour into the bowl. Mix well, then add the quinoa and mix again. Season with pepper; the soy sauce is salty, so you won't need to add extra salt.

4 Sit the tomato shells on a baking sheet. Spoon the quinoa mixture into the tomatoes, drizzle with the olive oil, and bake in a preheated oven, at 375°F, for 30-35 minutes, until the tomatoes are tender.

TEMPEH & QUINOA SUPERFOOD BOWL

1¼ cups black, red, or white quinoa
1¼ cups water
1 teaspoon vegan bouillon powder
2 cups diagonally sliced sugar
   snap peas or snow peas
1½ cups shredded kale
7 oz tempeh
1 tablespoon olive oil
3 tablespoons pumpkin seeds
¼ cup chopped chives
⅓ cup almonds, cashew nuts,
   or peanuts
⅓ cup golden raisins

Dressing
3 tablespoons tahini
1 garlic clove, crushed
½ cup soy yogurt
2 teaspoons sugar
1 teaspoon vegan wine vinegar
   or lemon juice
salt and pepper

Serves **2-3**
Prep time **10 minutes**
Cooking time **20 minutes**

1 Put the quinoa into a saucepan with the measured water and the bouillon powder. Cook gently for about 10 minutes, until the quinoa is tender and the liquid is absorbed. Place the sugar snaps or snow peas and kale on top. Cover with a lid and cook gently for another 5 minutes, until the vegetables are tender. Transfer to a bowl.

2 Place the tempeh between several sheets of paper towels and squeeze out the moisture. Heat the oil in a skillet and cook the tempeh on both sides for about 3-4 minutes, until golden. Add the pumpkin seeds and cook for another 30 seconds, or until they start to pop. Slice the tempeh and add to the bowl along with the seeds.

3 For the dressing, put all the ingredients into a bowl and beat well with a handheld mixer or wire balloon whisk until thick and smooth. Stir the chives, nuts, and golden raisins into the salad and serve with spoonfuls of the dressing.

AFFORDABILITY 2

PEA & MINT PESTO
FETTUCCINE

8 oz dried egg-free fettuccine
1²/₃ cups frozen peas, defrosted
1 garlic clove, coarsely chopped
1 teaspoon wasabi
¹/₃ cup mint
¹/₃ cup olive oil
2 tablespoons pine nuts
²/₃ cup water
salt and pepper
mint leaves, to garnish

Serves **4**
Prep time **20 minutes**
Cooking time **10-12 minutes**

1 Cook the fettuccine in a large saucepan of lightly salted boiling water for 8-10 minutes, or according to package directions, until just tender.

2 Meanwhile, blend together the peas, garlic, wasabi, mint, oil, pine nuts, and measured water in a blender or food processor until well combined. Season with plenty of salt and pepper.

3 Drain the pasta well and return to the pan with the pea pesto. Toss over gentle heat for 2-3 minutes, until piping hot.

4 Sprinkle with the mint and serve immediately in warm serving bowls with crusty bread.

VARIATION

For basil pesto with fettuccine, cook 12 oz dried egg-free fettuccine as above. Meanwhile, blend together 1 whole garlic clove, 2 handfuls of basil leaves, ¹/₃ cup of olive oil, and 3 tablespoons of pine nuts in a blender or food processor until smooth. Season well with salt and pepper. Drain the pasta well and return to the pan with the basil pesto. Toss over gentle heat for 1-2 minutes, until piping hot, then serve immediately in warm serving bowls.

AFFORDABILITY
2

PASTA *with* ROMESCO SAUCE

5 oz fusilli or penne pasta
2 slices vegan white bread
3 tablespoons olive oil
2 pointed red bell peppers, cored, seeded, and chopped
⅓ cup slivered almonds
3 tablespoons chopped parsley
1 red chili, seeded and finely chopped
2 garlic cloves, finely chopped
1 teaspoon vegan bouillon powder
2 tablespoons tomato paste
2 teaspoons vegan white or red wine vinegar
1 cup water
salt and pepper

Serves **2**
Prep time **10 minutes**
Cooking time **20 minutes**

1 Bring a saucepan of salted water to a boil and cook the pasta for about 12 minutes or according to package directions, until tender.

2 Make fresh coarse bread crumbs from the bread, either in a food processor or by grating using a box grater.

3 Heat 1 tablespoon of the oil in a skillet and sauté the bell peppers for 6-8 minutes, until softened and beginning to brown. Lift out onto a plate and add the remaining oil, the almonds, and bread crumbs to the pan. Cook gently for a couple of minutes, stirring frequently until the crumbs begin to brown. Spoon 3 tablespoons of the mixture onto a plate, stir in the parsley, and set aside.

4 Return the bell peppers to the pan with the chili, garlic, bouillon powder, tomato paste, vinegar, and measured water. Cook, stirring frequently, for 5 minutes, until thick and pulpy, adding a dash more water if the mixture becomes too dry.

5 Drain the pasta and return to the saucepan. Add the red pepper sauce and mix well to combine. Transfer to serving plates and sprinkle the parsley crumbs on top.

Pasta
WITH TOMATO & BASIL SAUCE

1. Cook the pasta in a large saucepan of salted boiling water according to the package directions.

2. Meanwhile, heat 1 tablespoon of the oil in a skillet, add the garlic, and cook over low heat for 1 minute. As soon as the garlic begins to brown, remove the pan from the heat and add the remaining oil.

3. Drain the pasta and return to the pan. Add the garlic oil with the tomatoes and basil. Season to taste with salt and pepper and toss well to mix. Serve immediately.

14 oz dried spaghetti
1/3 cup olive oil
5 garlic cloves, finely chopped
6 ripe tomatoes, seeded and chopped
2/3 cup basil leaves
salt and pepper

Serves **4**
Prep time **10 minutes**
Cooking time **10 minutes**

CHICKPEA
MINESTRONE
WITH ARUGULA

1 Heat the oil in a large, deep saucepan, add the onion, and cook over medium-high heat for 3–4 minutes, until beginning to soften. Add the garlic and cook, stirring, for 1 minute.

2 Add the chickpeas, green beans, and tomatoes to the pan and stir well, then stir in the broth, tomato juice, and pasta. Bring to a boil, then cover and simmer for 15 minutes, until the pasta is tender.

3 Remove the lid and continue to cook for another 10 minutes, adding three-quarters of the arugula and the parsley just before the end of cooking and stirring through. Season generously with salt and pepper.

4 Serve in warm serving bowls with the remaining arugula sprinkled over the top to garnish, along with warm crusty whole-wheat bread.

2 tablespoons olive oil
1 red onion, finely chopped
1 garlic clove, sliced
1 (15 oz) can chickpeas (garbanzo beans), drained and rinsed
1½ cups trimmed and diagonally sliced green beans
16 cherry tomatoes
3¾ cups) vegetable broth (see page 219)
1¼ cups tomato juice
5 oz dried whole-wheat pasta shapes
3½ cups wild arugula
⅓ cup chopped flat leaf parsley
salt and pepper

Serves **4**
Prep time **20 minutes**
Cooking time **30 minutes**

AFFORDABILITY

Caper, Lemon & Chili
SPAGHETTI

12 oz spelt spaghetti
2¼ cups baby broccoli pieces
2 tablespoons olive oil
1 small red onion, thinly sliced
1 red chili, seeded and chopped
2 tablespoons capers
finely grated zest of 1 lemon and
    1 tablespoon juice
2 tablespoons balsamic vinegar
salt and pepper

Serves **4**
Prep time **5 minutes**
Cooking time **12 minutes**

1 Cook the spaghetti in a large saucepan of salted boiling water for 10 minutes, or according to package directions, adding the baby broccoli for the final 3 minutes or until just tender.

2 Meanwhile, heat the oil in a skillet, add the onion and chili, and cook over gentle heat for 2 minutes. Stir in the capers, lemon zest and juice, and vinegar, season with salt and pepper, and heat through.

3 Drain the spaghetti and broccoli, reserving 1 tablespoon of the cooking water and adding it to the caper mixture. Add the drained spaghetti and broccoli to the pan and toss well to combine over the heat. Serve with an extra grinding of black pepper.

VARIATION

For artichoke, lemon & mint spaghetti, cook 12 oz spaghetti as above, adding 1 cup frozen peas for the final 3 minutes, until just tender. Meanwhile, heat 2 tablespoons of olive oil in a skillet, add 12 drained marinated artichokes in oil from a jar, and heat through for 1 minute. Stir in the finely grated zest of 1 lemon, 1 tablespoon of lemon juice, and 2 tablespoons each of balsamic vinegar and chopped mint, and season with salt and pepper. Drain the spaghetti and peas, reserving 1 tablespoon of the cooking water and adding it to the artichoke mixture. Add the drained spaghetti and peas to the pan and toss well to combine over the heat. Serve with an extra grinding of pepper.

AFFORDABILITY 2

CHILI & AVOCADO
PASTA BOWL

6 oz spinach fusilli or other
   pasta shapes
1 large ripe avocado
2 tablespoons olive oil
2 scallions, chopped
½ red chili, seeded and finely
   chopped
2 tablespoons sweet chili sauce
1 tomato, diced
small handful cilantro, chopped
lime wedges, to serve

Serves **2**
Prep time **10 minutes**
Cooking time **10 minutes**

1 Cook the pasta in boiling, lightly salted water for about
   10 minutes, or according to package direcitons, until tender.

2 Halve and pit the avocado. Scoop one half into a bowl and
   thoroughly mash with the oil. Beat in the scallions, chili,
   chili sauce, and tomato. Dice the remaining avocado.

3 Drain the pasta and return to the pan. Stir in the avocado
   sauce and diced avocado. Transfer to serving bowls and
   sprinkle with the cilantro. Serve with lime wedges for
   squeezing over.

STUDENT TIP

STEAMING GREENS Get into the habit of steaming
instead of boiling vegetables. They will taste better
and you won't lose all the valuable nutrients in the
cooking water. You don't need an expensive steamer;
you can use a metal colander over a pan of simmering
water, covered with a lid to keep the steam in.

MIXED MUSHROOM
Ragu sauce

1. Put the dried mushrooms into a bowl and pour over enough hot water to cover. Let soak for 20 minutes.

2. Heat the oil in a large saucepan, add the onion, celery, carrot, and garlic, and cook over low heat for 8 minutes, stirring occasionally, until softened. Increase the heat, stir in the fresh mushrooms, and cook for 3-4 minutes.

3. Strain the soaked dried mushrooms through a strainer, reserving the liquid. Add the dried mushrooms to the pan.

4. Pour in the broth or wine, bring to a boil, and cook until reduced by half. Stir in the reserved soaking liquid, tomatoes, tomato paste, vinegar, and oregano, season with salt and pepper, and bring to a boil.

5. Reduce the heat, cover, and simmer for 40-50 minutes, until the sauce is thick and the mushrooms are tender.

6. Meanwhile, cook the spaghetti in a large saucepan of lightly salted boiling water for 8-10 minutes, or according to package directions, until al dente. Drain and serve immediately topped with the mushroom sauce and grated cheese.

1 oz dried wild mushrooms, such as porcini and chanterelle
2 tablespoons olive oil
1 large onion, chopped
1 celery stalk, finely chopped
1 carrot, finely chopped
2 garlic cloves, crushed
1 lb mixed mushrooms, trimmed and coarsely chopped
$^2/_3$ cup vegetable broth (see page 219) or vegan red wine
1 (14½ oz) can diced tomatoes
1 tablespoon tomato paste
1 teaspoon balsamic vinegar
2 teaspoons dried oregano
10 oz dried spaghetti
salt and pepper
grated Parmesan-style vegan cheese, to serve

Serves **4**
Prep time **20 minutes, plus soaking**
Cooking time **1-1 ¼ hours**

AFFORDABILITY
3

TAGLIATELLE
with Squash & Sage

1 Put the squash into a small roasting pan, add half the olive oil, season, and toss to mix well. Roast in a preheated oven, at 425°F, for 15-20 minutes or until just tender.

2 Meanwhile, bring a large saucepan of salted water to a boil. Cook the pasta according to the package directions. Drain, return to the pan, then add the arugula, sage, and roasted squash. Mix together over gentle heat with the remaining olive oil until the arugula has wilted, then serve with a good grating of Parmesan-style vegan cheese, if desired.

1 (1¾ lb) butternut squash or other winter squash, peeled, seeded, and cut into ¾ inch cubes
¼ cup olive oil
1 lb fresh tagliatelle
2½ cups arugula leaves
8 sage leaves, chopped
salt and pepper

Serves **4**
Prep time **10 minutes**
Cooking time **20 minutes**

AFFORDABILITY
1

BUTTERNUT SQUASH & FRIED SAGE
Linguini

1. Slice the squash across into ¾ inch slices. Discard the seeds and cut away the skin. Chop the flesh into small pieces and sprinkle in a roasting pan with the onions. Drizzle with 2 tablespoons of the oil and roast in a preheated oven, at 400°F, for 35-40 minutes, turning halfway through cooking, until tender and pale golden.

2. Heat the remaining oil in a large saucepan and add one sage leaf to see if the oil is hot enough for the sage to sizzle; if necessary, heat the oil a little more. Add the remaining leaves and cook for about 30 seconds, until crisped and lightly browned. Stir in the garlic, then transfer to a small bowl, including the oil.

3. Wipe out the saucepan, then fill with plenty of water and bring to a boil. Cook the linguini for about 10 minutes, or according to the package directions, until tender. Scoop out a small ladleful or cup of the liquid and drain the pasta.

4. Return to the pan with the reserved liquid and add the roasted vegetables, sage, garlic, oil, and cheese. Mix well and pile onto serving plates, sprinkling with extra cheese.

---

1 medium butternut squash
2 red onions, thinly sliced
¼ cup mild olive oil
20 fresh sage leaves
2 garlic cloves, finely chopped
5 oz linguini
½ cup shredded cheddar-style vegan cheese, plus extra to sprinkle

---

Serves **2**
Prep time **15 minutes**
Cooking time **40 minutes**

AFFORDABILITY
1

GNOCCHI
IN TOMATO & LEEK SAUCE

5 floury potatoes (about 1¼ lb),
  such as russet or Yukon Gold,
  scrubbed
1 cup all-purpose flour
salt and pepper

Sauce
1 tablespoon olive oil
1 leek, trimmed, cleaned and
  chopped
1 garlic clove, crushed
4 ripe tomatoes, coarsely chopped
1 tablespoon tomato paste
pinch of sugar
small handful of torn basil leaves
salt and pepper

Serves **4**
Prep time **30 minutes**
Cooking time **25 minutes**

1 Cook the potatoes in their skins in a large saucepan of salted boiling water for about 20 minutes, until tender. Drain and let stand until cool enough to handle but not cold.

2 Meanwhile, make the sauce. Heat the oil in a skillet, add the leek, and cook over medium heat for 5 minutes, until tender. Add the garlic and tomatoes and cook for 5 minutes, until the tomatoes are soft. Stir in the tomato paste and a little water to make a sauce. Add the sugar, season with salt and pepper, and simmer for 3 minutes.

3 Peel the potatoes and pass them through a potato ricer or mash with a potato masher until smooth. Season with salt and pepper, then knead in the flour to form a dough.

4 Divide the gnocchi dough into 4 pieces and roll each piece into a thick rope. Cut into ¾ inch pieces and press with the prongs of a fork to mark a ridged pattern.

5 Cook the gnocchi in a large saucepan of salted boiling water for 1-2 minutes, until they float to the surface. Remove from the pan with a slotted spoon and add to the sauce. Add the basil and gently turn the gnocchi to coat in the sauce. Serve with an extra grinding of pepper.

VARIATION

For fried gnocchi with broccoli & lemon, make the gnocchi as above (or use store-bought vegan gnocchi). Cook 2 cups broccoli florets in a saucepan of boiling salted water for 3 minutes, until just tender, then drain. Meanwhile, heat 3 tablespoons of olive oil in a large skillet, add the gnocchi, and cook for 8-10 minutes, until golden and crisp. Stir in 1 chopped red chili, 1 crushed garlic clove, the finely grated zest of 1 lemon, and the broccoli, and heat through for 3 minutes.

PEARL BARLEY RISOTTO WITH CARROTS

AFFORDABILITY
1

1 cup pearl barley
14 oz baby carrots, scrubbed
1/3 cup olive oil
1 large onion, finely chopped
1 large leek, trimmed, cleaned,
    and thinly sliced
1 garlic clove, thinly sliced
1 tablespoon thyme leaves
1 teaspoon ground coriander
5 cups vegetable broth (see
    page 219), plus extra if needed
2 tablespoons chopped flat leaf
    parsley, to garnish
salt and pepper

Serves **4**
Prep time **15 minutes,**
    plus standing
Cooking time **25 minutes**

1 Put the pearl barley into a bowl, pour over enough boiling water to cover, and let stand for 10 minutes.

2 Toss the carrots in a shallow roasting pan with 2 tablespoons of the oil until evenly coated, then roast in a preheated oven, at 400°F, for 20 minutes, until tender and lightly charred in places.

3 Meanwhile, heat the remaining oil in a skillet, add the onion and leek with the garlic and thyme, and cook over medium heat, stirring occasionally, for 4 minutes, until soft and pale golden. Stir in the ground coriander and cook for another 1 minute.

4 Drain the pearl barley, add to the skillet with half the broth, and bring to a boil. Cover and simmer gently, stirring occasionally, for about 10 minutes, until almost all the broth is absorbed. Add the remaining broth and stir, then cover and simmer gently again until the pearl barleyis tender and some of the broth is still left in the pan, adding more broth, if necessary.

5 Add the roasted carrots to the risotto and stir through. Season and serve with warm whole-wheat bread.

VARIATION
For roasted root vegetable risotto, put 7 oz scrubbed baby carrots into a roasting pan with 2 parsnips, peeled and cut into sticks, and 1 large turnip, peeled and chopped. Add 3 tablespoons of olive oil and toss. Add 1 tablespoon of chopped rosemary leaves and toss again. Roast in a preheated oven, at 400°F, for 20-25 minutes, until lightly charred and tender. Meanwhile, cook the onion, leek, and garlic as above, omitting the thyme, then add and cook the pearl barley as above. Fold in the roasted veggies and season.

TOFU
& VEGETABLE FRIED RICE

AFFORDABILITY 2

1 Spray a large nonstick wok or skillet with cooking spray and heat over high heat. Add the onion and stir-fry for 1-2 minutes, until slightly softened. Add the garlic and chili and stir-fry for about 1 minute, until aromatic.

2 Add the carrot, baby corn, bok choy stems, and tomatoes to the pan and stir-fry for about 3 minutes, until softened. Transfer to a bowl.

3 Wipe the pan clean with paper towels, respray with cooking spray, and heat over high heat. Add the cooked rice and stir-fry for 3-4 minutes, until piping hot. Add the bok choy leaves, sweet chili sauce, and soy sauce with the reserved vegetables and toss together briefly until heated through. Remove from the heat and stir in the tofu and herbs. Ladle into warm bowls and serve.

cooking spray
1 red onion, cut into thin wedges
2 garlic cloves, finely chopped
1 red chili, seeded and finely chopped
1 carrot, cut into thin matchsticks
12 baby corn, diagonally sliced
1 bunch of bok choy, stems and leaves separated
16 cherry tomatoes, halved
2½ cups freshly cooked long-grain rice, cooled
2 tablespoons sweet chili sauce
2 tablespoons light soy sauce
7 oz firm tofu, drained and cut into bite-size cubes
large handful of cilantro and mint, finely chopped

Serves **4**
Prep time **15 minutes**
Cooking time **15 minutes**

GINGER & TOFU
Sweet & Sour

1 Make the tamarind paste, if using. Soak 2 tablespoons tamarind pulp in 1 cup boiling water for 4-5 minutes. Mash with a spoon or fork to help it dissolve. Then strain the thick liquid into a small bowl and reserve the fibers in another bowl (use these if you need to strain the liquid again).

2 Heat 2 inches of oil in a wok over medium heat. Deep-fry the ginger without stirring for 6-8 minutes. Remove the ginger with a slotted spoon, then drain on paper towels.

3 Lower the tofu into the oil, in batches, and deep-fry for 5-6 minutes, until lightly browned and soft inside. Drain on paper towels.

4 Remove most of the oil, leaving 1½ tablespoons in the wok. Stir-fry the garlic over medium heat for 1-2 minutes or until lightly browned. Add the sugar, soy sauce, broth or water, and tamarind paste or lime juice, and stir over low heat until slightly thickened. Taste and adjust the seasoning. Add the tofu and most of the crispy ginger and mix together.

5 Spoon into 4 warm serving bowls and garnish with the remainder of the crispy ginger.

3 tablespoons tamarind paste
  or 2 tablespoons lime juice
sunflower oil, for deep-frying
3 cups finely shredded fresh
  ginger root
1 lb 2 oz firm tofu, drained and
  cut into ½ inch cubes
2 garlic cloves, finely chopped
¼ cup packed coconut sugar or
  brown sugar
2 tablespoons light soy sauce
2 tablespoons vegetable broth
  (see page 219) or water

Serves **4**
Prep time **15 minutes**
Cooking time **30-40 minutes**

Crunchy nut stir-fry
ON MASHED SWEET POTATO & MISO

3 sweet potatoes, scrubbed and cut into small chunks
2 tablespoons vegetable oil
1 (12 oz) package mixed stir-fry vegetables, including bean sprouts
½ bunch scallions, chopped
2 cups shredded collard greens
2 tablespoons white or brown miso paste
3 tablespoons rice or almond milk
⅓ cup salted peanuts
1 tablespoon soy sauce
2 teaspoons rice wine vinegar or vegan wine vinegar

Serves **2**
Prep time **10 minutes**
Cooking time **10 minutes**

1 Cook the potatoes in boiling water for 8-10 minutes or until tender.

2 Meanwhile, heat the oil in a skillet or wok and add the stir-fry vegetables, scallions, and collard greens. Cook, stirring, for 3-4 minutes, until slightly softened.

3 Drain the sweet potatoes and return to the saucepan. Mash well and beat in the miso paste and milk.

4 Spoon the mashed sweet potatoes onto serving plates and spread out a little with the back of the spoon. Stir the peanuts into the stir-fry and heat through briefly. Turn out onto the sweet potatoes to serve and drizzle the soy sauce and vinegar on top.

AFFORDABILITY
3

NOODLE & VEGETABLE *Stir-fry*

1 Soak the rice noodles in boiling water for 4 minutes, then rinse in cold water and drain.

2 Heat a wok or large skillet until hot, add the coconut oil, then add the onion and tofu. Stir briskly to sear on all sides until golden.

3 Pour in the soy sauce and stir to coat the mixture. Reduce the heat and add the remaining ingredients along with the drained noodles, stirring until hot.

4 Transfer the stir-fry to warm serving bowls, sprinkle with nori flakes and sesame seeds, and serve with a wedge of lime, if you want.

2 oz rice noodles
2 teaspoons coconut oil
1 red onion, sliced
8 oz tofu
2 tablespoons soy sauce
1 teaspoon finely chopped fresh
    ginger root
1 garlic clove, finely chopped
1⅓ cups finely sliced cabbage
1 ⅓ cups bean sprouts
8 lychees, peeled, pitted, and
    quartered
2 teaspoons blackstrap molasses

To serve
nori flakes
sesame seeds
lime wedges (optional)

Serves **2**
Prep time **10 minutes**
Cooking time **10 minutes**

BALANCING ACT

A vegan diet can be healthy, nutritious, and satisfying, but it requires extra thought and effort—especially when you're shopping for, and preparing, all your own meals. Because you won't be getting quick-fix protein hits from animal-based ingredients, such as meat, eggs, and fish, and a daily calcium boost from dairy, you need to boost your intake from other sources. Student life can be hectic, so vegans need to be extra careful to be sure they're eating a balanced diet.

STOCK UP ON SNACKS
Keep a supply of dried fruit, nuts, and seeds on hand so there's always something nutritious to grab, whatever your time constraints. A good stock of zip-top food bags and small plastic food containers makes it easy to snack on the go.

FRUIT AND VEGGIE
Whether you're vegan or not, the latest advice is to try to get your consumption of fresh fruit and veg closer to ten servings a day. Vegans are usually pretty good at including these in their diet, but remember to choose a selection of different colors when shopping to get the most vitamins and other nutrients into your daily diet.

LOAD UP ON CARBS AT MEALTIMES

Rice, pasta, and potatoes are prime sources of carbohydrates, and you should try to include a hearty serving with each meal. They will give you energy and keep you full between meals.

DAIRY ALTERNATIVES

Include soy, rice, oat, and other dairy alternatives in your meals and snacks to make sure you get enough calcium in your diet. Tofu is another good source, so add it to your shopping list, too.

PUMPING IRON

Aim for dark green on the vegetable color chart. Broccoli, leafy vegetables, and watercress are all good ways to maximize your iron intake. And don't wash the good stuff away by boiling your veg: always steam it to keep the vitamins intact.

OMEGA-3

The main sources of omega-3 are oily fish, so you'll need to get your omega-3 fatty acids from other ingredients. Fortunately, soy, nuts, and canola oil are all vegan-friendly and high in omega-3s.

KEEP HYDRATED

Water has a vital part to play in helping you stay alert, focused, and full of energy, as well as helping to rid your body of unwanted pollutants. Keep a bottle in your bag and on your desk, and down a glass of water every time you're waiting to make a cup of coffee or tea.

Malaysian COCONUT & VEGETABLE STEW

2 tablespoons vegetable oil
1 medium onion, thinly sliced
⅓ cup laksa curry paste
3⅓ cups coconut milk
1 teaspoon salt
1¼ cups water
2 potatoes, peeled and cut into
 ¾ inch pieces
4 carrots, peeled and cut into
 ¾ inch pieces
1 cup trimmed and halved
 green beans
1 cup cauliflower florets
½ butternut squash, peeled,
 seeded, and cut into ¾ inch
 cubes
⅓ cup cashew nuts
½ cup bean sprouts
4 scallions, trimmed and sliced
 on the diagonal
handful of Thai sweet basil leaves
 or fresh cilantro

Serves **4**
Prep time **5 minutes**
Cooking time **25 minutes**

1 Heat the oil in a large saucepan over medium heat. Add the onion and curry paste and sauté gently for 2-3 minutes, until it begins to smell fragrant.

2 Add the coconut milk, salt, and measured water and bring to a boil.

3 Add the potatoes and carrots and cook for 10 minutes, then add the green beans, cauliflower, and squash and cook for another 7 minutes.

4 Add the cashew nuts and simmer for 3 minutes, until the vegetables are just tender.

5 Stir in the bean sprouts, scallions, and basil or cilantro. Simmer for 1 minute and serve immediately.

THAI GREEN
Vegetable Curry

1. Peel and slice the hard winter squash and cut into 1 inch cubes. Quarter the eggplants and slice the zucchini and mushrooms. Cut the asparagus into 1 inch pieces and trim the ends off the beans. Cook the hard winter squash in boiling water over medium heat for 8-10 minutes or until soft, then drain.

2. Heat the oil in a wok or saucepan. Stir-fry the curry paste and goji berries, if using, over medium heat for 3-4 minutes, until fragrant. Add the eggplants, zucchini, and mushrooms and stir-fry for 4-5 minutes. Add the asparagus, corn, and green beans and gently stir-fry for another 2-3 minutes.

3. Add the soy milk, soy sauce, sugar, cooked hard winter squash, and pineapple and warm through for 2-3 minutes, stirring occasionally. Taste and adjust the seasoning.

4. Spoon into 4 serving bowls and garnish with Thai sweet basil leaves and chili slices.

7 oz mixed winter squash, such as butternut squash, acorn squash, pattypan squash, or pumpkin (about 1½ cups prepared)
8 oz mixed soft vegetables, such as Thai eggplants, baby corn, zucchini, mushrooms, asparagus, and green beans (about 1½ cups prepared)
1½-2 tablespoons sunflower oil
2-3 tablespoons Thai green curry paste
25 sun-dried goji berries (optional)
2 cups soy milk
3 tablespoons light soy sauce
1 tablespoon packed coconut or brown sugar
1 cup pineapple chunks (fresh or canned in light juices)

To garnish
Thai sweet basil, leaves picked
few slices of red chilli

Serves **4**
Prep time **15 minutes**
Cooking time **25 minutes**

STUDENT TIP

WEEKLY SHOPPING Although it's tempting to add to your weekly groceries by stopping at a convenience store on the way home from college, you'll pay more for the privilege. Instead, plan out your weekly shopping before going to a larger grocery store or supermarket to get the best prices and bargains.

AFFORDABILITY
2

CHICKPEA & SPINACH STEW

1 Put the chickpeas into a deep bowl and cover with cold water. Let soak overnight.

2 Transfer to a colander and rinse under cold running water. Drain and put into a saucepan. Cover with water and bring to a boil, then reduce the heat to low. Simmer gently for 45 minutes, skimming off any scum that rises to the surface and stirring often. Drain and set aside.

3 Meanwhile, heat the oil in a wok, add the onions, and cook over low heat for 15 minutes, until lightly golden. Add the coriander, cumin, chili powder, turmeric, and curry powder and stir-fry for 1-2 minutes. Add the tomatoes, sugar, and measured water and bring to a boil. Cover, reduce the heat, and simmer gently for 15 minutes.

4 Add the chickpeas, season to taste, and cook gently for 8-10 minutes. Stir in the mint. Divide the spinach leaves among 4 shallow bowls and top with the chickpea mixture. Serve immediately with steamed rice or bread.

1 cup dried chickpeas
   (garbanzo beans)
1 tablespoon peanut oil
2 onions, thinly sliced
2 teaspoons ground coriander
2 teaspoons ground cumin
1 teaspoon hot chili powder
1/2 teaspoon ground turmeric
1 tablespoon medium curry
   powder
1 (14 1/2 oz) can diced tomatoes
1 teaspoon packed brown sugar
1/2 cup water
2 tablespoons chopped mint
3 1/2 cups baby spinach
salt

Serves **4**
Prep time **20 minutes,
   plus soaking**
Cooking time **1 hour**

AFFORDABILITY
1

BLACK LENTIL *Stew*

1 Put the lentils into a deep bowl and cover with cold water. Let soak for 10-12 hours. Transfer to a colander and rinse under cold running water. Drain and put into a saucepan with half the measured water. Bring to a boil, reduce the heat to low, and simmer for 35-40 minutes, until tender. Drain and set aside.

2 Heat the oil in a large saucepan over medium heat. Add the onion, garlic, ginger, chili, cumin seeds, and ground coriander, and stir-fry for 5-6 minutes, until the onion is soft and translucent. Add the turmeric, paprika, kidney beans, and cooked lentils, and stir thoroughly.

3 Add the remaining measured water and bring back to a boil. Reduce the heat to low and simmer gently for 10-15 minutes, stirring often. Remove from the heat and season to taste. Stir in the cilantro and sprinkle with a little extra paprika. Serve immediately with the yogurt.

²/₃ cup dried whole black lentils, rinsed and drained
4 cups water
1 tablespoon peanut oil
1 onion, finely chopped
3 garlic cloves, crushed
2 teaspoons peeled and finely grated fresh ginger root
1 fresh green chili, halved lengthwise
2 teaspoons cumin seeds
1 teaspoon ground coriander
1 teaspoon ground turmeric
1 teaspoon paprika, plus extra for sprinkling
1¹/₃ cups rinsed and drained, canned red kidney beans
large handful of chopped cilantro
salt
1 cup soy yogurt, whisked, to serve

Serves **4**
Prep time **20 minutes, plus soaking**
Cooking time **about 1 hour**

AFFORDABILITY

Okra, Pea & Tomato
STEW

1 tablespoon peanut oil
6-8 curry leaves
2 teaspoons black mustard seeds
1 onion, finely diced
2 teaspoons ground cumin
1 teaspoon ground coriander
2 teaspoons curry powder
1 teaspoon ground turmeric
3 garlic cloves, finely chopped
2 cups diagonally sliced, 1 inch
  okra pieces
1⅓ cups fresh or frozen peas
2 ripe plum tomatoes, finely
  chopped
salt and pepper
3 tablespoons grated fresh
  coconut, to serve

Serves **4**
Prep time **5 minutes**
Cooking time **about 20 minutes**

1 Heat the oil in a large nonstick wok or skillet over medium heat. Add the curry leaves, mustard seeds, and onion. Stir-fry for 3-4 minutes, until fragrant and the onion is starting to soften, then add the cumin, coriander, curry powder, and turmeric. Stir-fry for another 1-2 minutes, until fragrant.

2 Add the garlic and okra, and increase the heat to high. Cook, stirring, for 2-3 minutes, then add the peas and tomatoes. Season to taste, cover, and reduce the heat to low. Cook gently for 10-12 minutes, stirring occasionally, until the okra is just tender. Remove from the heat and sprinkle with the grated coconut just before serving.

VARIATION
For spicy pea & tomato pilaf with seeds, put 1⅔ cups basmati rice or other long-grain rice into a medium saucepan with 2 teaspoons of dry-roasted cumin seeds, 1 tablespoon of crushed dry-roasted coriander seeds, 2 teaspoons of black mustard seeds, 1⅓ cups fresh or frozen peas, and 3 peeled, seeded, and finely diced tomatoes. Add 2¾ cups boiling vegetable broth, bring to a boil, and season to taste. Reduce the heat to low, cover the pan and cook gently for 10-12 minutes or until all the liquid has been absorbed. Remove from the heat and let stand, covered and undisturbed, for 10-15 minutes. Fluff up the grains with a fork and serve.

WILD RICE, PARSNIP & PEANUT *Stew*

AFFORDABILITY
2

¾ cup wild rice, rinsed
3 tablespoons vegetable oil
2 onions, thinly sliced
3 garlic cloves, finely chopped
1 tablespoon vegan bouillon
  powder
1 tablespoon vegan hot
  curry paste
1 teaspoon ground turmeric
3⅓ cups boiling water
4 parsnips (about 1 lb), cut into
  small chunks
8 pieces baby broccoli, stems cut
  into ½ inch lengths
3 tablespoons chunky
  peanut butter
3 tablespoons chopped cilantro
⅓ cup coarsely chopped
  salted peanuts
salt and pepper

Serves **4**
Prep time **15 minutes**
Cooking time **55 minutes**

1 Cook the wild rice in plenty of boiling water for about 30 minutes, or according to package directions, until the grains have softened but have not lost their shape. Drain.

2 Meanwhile, heat the oil in a large saucepan and gently sauté the onions for 10 minutes, until softened and golden. Stir in the garlic and cook for another 1 minute. Add the bouillon powder, curry paste, and turmeric, and stir in the measured boiling water. Add the parsnips and bring to a gentle simmer. Cover with a lid and cook for 20 minutes.

3 Add the rice and broccoli and cook for another 20 minutes, until the rice and vegetables are tender.

4 Ladle a little of the broth into a heatproof bowl or mug and stir in the peanut butter until softened. Add to the stew and stir well until heated through. Season to taste with salt and pepper and ladle into bowls. Serve sprinkled with the cilantro and peanuts.

SPICY GOAN EGGPLANT SLICES

1. Dry-roast the cumin and coriander seeds in a nonstick skillet over low heat for 2-3 minutes, until fragrant.

2. Remove from the heat and crush them lightly. Transfer to a large saucepan with the chilies, turmeric, cayenne, garlic, ginger, and measured warm water.

3. Bring to a boil, reduce the heat, and simmer for 10 minutes, until thickened. Season to taste. Stir in the coconut milk and tamarind paste.

4. Arrange the eggplant slices in a foil-lined broiler pan and brush with some of the coconut milk sauce. Cook under a preheated hot broiler, turning once, until golden and tender. Add the eggplant slices to the sauce, gently heat, and serve with vegan flatbread.

VARIATION

For cashew & zucchini slices, add 1²/₃ cups roasted cashew nuts to the finished stew. To roast the nuts, soak in water for 20 minutes, then heat in a dry skillet, shaking regularly, until lightly browned before chopping them. Replace the eggplant with 4 sliced zucchini and broil as above. Drizzle with walnut oil and season to taste before adding to the stew.

1 teaspoon cumin seeds
4 teaspoons coriander seeds
2 fresh green chilies, seeded and sliced
½ teaspoon ground turmeric
1 teaspoon cayenne pepper
4 garlic cloves, crushed
1 tablespoon peeled and grated fresh ginger root
1¼ cups warm water
1²/₃ cups coconut milk
1 tablespoon tamarind paste
1 large eggplant, thinly sliced lengthwise
salt and pepper

Serves **4**
Prep time **15 minutes**
Cooking time **25 minutes**

MILD COCONUT STEW

1. Put the potatoes, lemongrass, and lentils into a medium saucepan and add enough water to just cover the tops of the potatoes. Bring to a boil, then simmer for about 15 minutes.

2. Heat the oil in a large saucepan and sauté the onion, garlic, mushrooms, turmeric, and cumin until the onion is soft. Add all the remaining ingredients, except for the cilantro, and stir well.

3. Remove the lemongrass from the lentil pan, then add the lentils and potatoes to the onion mixture.

4. Simmer everything for about 10 minutes or until the lentils are soft, then add the chopped cilantro.

5. Serve with brown basmati rice cooked with a few cardamom pods, plus warm vegan flatbread.

2 medium potatoes, chopped
1 lemongrass stalk
¼ cup French green lentils
1 tablespoon coconut oil
1 onion, chopped
2 garlic cloves, chopped
6 mushrooms, sliced
1 teaspoon ground turmeric
1 teaspoon ground cumin
1 cup green beans
1 yellow bell pepper, cored, seeded, and chopped
1 zucchini, chopped
1½ cups frozen corn kernels
1¼ cups coconut milk
juice of 1 lime
1 tablespoon chopped cilantro

Serves **4**
Prep time **15 minutes**
Cooking time **30 minutes**

AFFORDABILITY
2

Jamaican-style
BEAN, ZUCCHINI & COCONUT
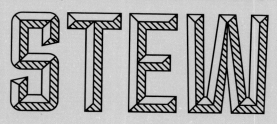

AFFORDABILITY 1

1. Heat the coconut oil in a large saucepan and gently sauté the onions for 5 minutes, stirring frequently. Add the zucchini and cook for another 8-10 minutes, until deep golden. Stir in the ginger, dried chilies, coriander seeds, mustard seeds, cayenne pepper, and turmeric and cook, stirring continuously, for 2 minutes. Add the garlic and cook for another 1 minute.

2. Add the black-eyed peas, coconut cream, broth, and sugar and bring to a gentle simmer. Cover with a lid and cook for 5 minutes.

3. Add the potatoes and continue to cook for 25-30 minutes, until all the vegetables are tender and the juices are thickened. Serve in bowls with lime wedges for drizzling.

3 tablespoons coconut oil
2 onions, chopped
3 zucchini (about 1 lb), cut into ½ inch chunks
¾ oz piece of fresh ginger root, finely chopped
¼ teaspoon crushed dried chilies
2 teaspoons coriander seeds, lightly crushed
1 tablespoon black or yellow mustard seeds
½ teaspoon cayenne pepper
1 teaspoon ground turmeric
2 garlic cloves, finely chopped
1 (15 oz) can black-eyed peas, drained and rinsed
⅔ cup coconut cream
1¼ cups vegetable broth (see page 219)
1 teaspoon light muscovado sugar
4 russet potatoes (about 1 lb), cut into ¾ inch chunks
lime wedges, to serve

Serves **4**
Prep time **20 minutes**
Cooking time **55 minutes**

STUDENT TIP

BEFRIEND YOUR FREEZER Whether it's freezing leftovers or making and freezing extra servings, you'll save time and money by stocking up on some future meals. Always label bags and containers, or dinner will be a lucky dip.

CAULIFLOWER & CHICKPEA
Pan-fry

1/3 cup olive oil
1 red onion, cut into thin wedges
1/2 cauliflower, cut into small florets
1 teaspoon garam masala
1 teaspoon ground coriander
1/4 cup cold water, plus 2/3 cup water
28 Swiss chard leaves, washed, patted dry, and cut into strips
1 teaspoon cumin seeds
1 garlic clove, thinly sliced
1 (15 oz) can chickpeas (garbanzo beans), drained and rinsed
1/3 cup tahini
1/4 cup lemon juice

salt and pepper
vegan flatbread, to serve

Serves **4**
Prep time **20 minutes**
Cooking time **20 minutes**

AFFORDABILITY
1

1 Heat the oil in a large, heavy skillet or wok, add the onion, and cook over medium-high heat, stirring frequently, for 3–4 minutes, until beginning to soften.

2 Add the cauliflower florets, garam masala, and coriander and cook for 5 minutes, stirring almost constantly to prevent the cauliflower from catching, then add the 1/4 cup cold water. Cook for another 2 minutes and keep stirring.

3 Stir the Swiss chard, cumin, and garlic into the pan and cook, stirring, for another 2 minutes. Add the chickpeas along with the tahini, lemon juice, and remaining 2/3 cup measured water, and season with salt and pepper. Toss the vegetables in the sauce, then reduce the heat, cover, and simmer for 2 minutes. Season generously with salt and pepper.

4 Toss again before serving in warm serving bowls with vegan flatbread, such as pita bread, naan, or chiapati.

VARIATION

For curried broccoli pan-fry with cumin seeds, heat 3 tablespoons of olive oil in a large, heavy skillet or wok, add 1 large white onion, thinly sliced into wedges, and stir-fry over medium-high heat for 2 minutes. Add 4 cups small broccoli florets and 1 red bell pepper, cored, seeded, and thinly sliced, and stir-fry for 3–4 minutes, until softened. Add 2 tablespoons of curry paste and 1 teaspoon of cumin seeds and cook, stirring, for another 1 minute. Add 2 tablespoons of mango chutney, season with salt and pepper, if necessary, and toss again for 1 minute. Serve piled onto 2 warm, halved vegan flatbreads.

TAKEOUT
ALTERNATIVES

The weekly takeout treat can be difficult for vegans. Many options are completely off-limits, while those that sound safe can't always be properly checked, because menus don't list the full ingredients. But don't let that put you off enjoying the same types of takeout dishes as your housemates. It's quick, easy—and a whole lot cheaper—to make your own takeout meals at home. Here are a few ideas to get you started.

INDIAN

Tarka dahl, a spicy lentil dish, is simple to make, and a big batch can be divided into individual servings. Serve with poppadoms (naturally dairy free) or naan (check it's dairy free—milk is often used in the ingredients). Another spicy vegan-friendly Indian dish is chana masala, made with spices and chickpeas (garbanzo beans). Sag aloo (spinach and potatoes), many rice dishes, and some baltis and biryanis are vegan, too.

CHINESE

When it comes to making your own Chinese takeout at home, tofu is your friend. So many Chinese dishes feature this tasty ingredient, simply cubed, fried, and cooked in sauce. Add a handful of cashew nuts for extra texture. Steamed Asian greens with seeds, stir-fried rice with peas, and vegetarian noodles will turn the meal into a banquet.

BURGER AND FRIES

Dairy-free buns are easy to find these days and the meat-free options for fillings are endless: lightly broil large portobello mushrooms, bell peppers, and soy meat alternatives and add vegan cheese, or thick slices of beefsteak tomatoes. And when it comes to fries, choose skin-on fries or wedges with plenty of dipping sauce and salt. Serve on paper plates to avoid washing dishes later on.

PIZZA

Vegan pizzas are available in some grocery stores (make sure the pizza crust is vegan, too), but it's easy to make your own pizza dough and top it with nondairy cheese, tomatoes, and other ingredients, such as olives, capers, bell peppers, corn kernels, and mushrooms. So, there's no need to miss out on this student favorite.

HOT DOGS

Instead of wolfing down hot dogs after a ball game, you can stuff vegan buns, tortilla wraps, pita bread, or other flatbreads with vegan frankfurters or another meat-free alternative, along with shredded iceberg, salsa, and/or chili sauce.

BLACK-EYED PEA &
RED PEPPER STEW

2 tablespoons olive oil
4 shallots, finely chopped
2 garlic cloves, crushed
2 celery stalks, diced
1 large carrot, peeled and cut into
 ½ inch pieces
1 red bell pepper, cored, seeded,
 and cut into ½ inch pieces
1 teaspoon dried mixed herbs
2 teaspoons ground cumin
1 teaspoon ground cinnamon
2 (14 ½ oz) cans diced tomatoes
2 tablespoons tomato paste
⅓ cup vegetable broth
 (see page 219)
2 (15 oz) cans black-eyed peas in
 water, drained and rinsed
¼ cup finely chopped cilantro
 leaves, plus extra to garnish
salt and pepper
cooked basmati rice, to serve

Serves **4**
Prep time **10 minutes**
Cooking time **20 minutes**

1 Heat the oil in a large skillet and put over high heat. Add the shallots, garlic, celery, carrot, and red bell pepper and stir-fry for 2–3 minutes or until lightly starting to brown.

2 Add the dried herbs, cumin, cinnamon, tomatoes, tomato paste, and broth and bring to a boil. Reduce the heat to medium, cover, and cook gently for 12–15 minutes or until the vegetables are tender, breaking up the tomatoes into small pieces with a wooden spoon toward the end of the cooking time.

3 Stir in the black-eyed peas and cook for 2–3 minutes or until piping hot.

4 Season well, remove from the heat, and sprinkle with the chopped cilantro. Garnish with cilantro leaves and serve with basmati rice.

PEPPER & LENTIL STEW
with Cornbread Muffins

1. Cook the lentils in boiling water for 20 minutes to soften. In a separate saucepan, melt the coconut oil and sauté the bell peppers and onion for about 12 minutes or until pale golden, stirring frequently. Add the garlic and cook for another 1 minute.

2. Stir in the Cajun spice, coconut milk, broth, and tomato paste. Drain the lentils, add to the pan of bell peppers, and bring to a simmer. Cook gently for 15 minutes.

3. For the muffins, line six sections of a muffin pan with paper muffin liners. Put the flour, cornmeal, baking powder, chili flakes, cheese, half the cilantro, and a little salt into a bowl and mix well.

4. In a small saucepan, melt the dairy-free spread over low heat and combine with the milk. Add the milk mixture to the bowl and stir with a blunt knife until the ingredients are just combined. Divide among the paper muffin liners.

5. Bake in a preheated oven, at 425°F, for 20 minutes, until risen and just beginning to brown. Stir the remaining cilantro into the bell peppers and lentils, heat through gently, and spoon into bowls. Serve with the muffins.

1 cup cooked or rinsed, canned green French lentils
2 tablespoons coconut oil
1 red bell pepper, cored, seeded, and cut into chunks
1 orange bell pepper, cored, seeded, and cut into chunks
1 green bell pepper, cored, seeded, and cut into chunks
2 onions, chopped
2 garlic cloves, crushed
1 tablespoon Cajun spice mix
1²/₃ cups coconut milk
1 cup vegetable broth (see page 219)
3 tablespoons tomato paste

Muffins
1 cup flour
1 cup cornmeal
2 teaspoons baking powder
½ teaspoon dried chili flakes
²/₃ cup shredded cheddar-style vegan cheese
½ cup chopped cilantro
3 tablespoons dairy-free spread
²/₃ cup rice or oat milk
salt

Serves **6**
Prep time **25 minutes**
Cooking time **1 hour**

QUICK VEGETABLE MOLE

1 Heat the oil in a large saucepan, add the onion and garlic, and cook over medium heat for 2–3 minutes, until softened. Add the sweet potatoes and red bell pepper and cook for another 2 minutes.

2 Stir in the chili powder, tomatoes, broth, and all the beans and bring to a boil. Reduce the heat, cover, and simmer gently for 20–25 minutes, until the vegetables are tender. Season to taste with salt and pepper.

3 Add the chocolate and cilantro and cook for another 2–3 minutes. Serve with long-grain rice topped with spoonfuls of plain soy yogurt, if you want.

VARIATION

For Mexican bean soup, heat 1 tablespoon of sunflower oil in a skillet, add 1 chopped onion, 1 chopped celery stalk, 2 diced carrots, and 1 cored, seeded, and chopped red bell pepper, and cook over medium heat for 5–6 minutes, until softened. Stir in 1 tablespoon of chili powder, 1 (14 ½ oz) can diced tomatoes, 1 (15 oz) can each of red kidney beans and black beans, drained and rinsed, and 2½ cups hot vegetable broth. Simmer for 10 minutes. Stir in 2 tablespoons grated semisweet dairy-free chocolate and serve in bowls, garnished with chopped scallions, chopped fresh cilantro, and a spoonful of plain soy yogurt.

1 tablespoon sunflower oil
1 large onion, chopped
1 garlic clove, crushed
3 sweet potatoes (about 1 lb), peeled and cut into small chunks
1 large red bell pepper, cored, seeded, and chopped
1 tablespoon chili powder
2 (14½ oz) cans diced tomatoes
²⁄₃ cup vegetable broth (see page 219)
1 (15 oz) can red kidney beans, drained and rinsed
1 (15 oz) can black beans, drained and rinsed
2 tablespoons grated dairy-free semisweet chocolate
2 tablespoons chopped fresh cilantro
salt and black pepper

Serves **4**
Prep time **10 minutes**
Cooking time **30–35 minutes**

AFFORDABILITY
1

SPINACH & MUSHROOM

Lasagne

1. Melt 1 tablespoon of the dairy-free spread in a large skillet or wide saucepan and sauté the onions and celery for 5 minutes. Add the mushrooms and sauté for another 10 minutes, until the mushrooms are lightly browned and all the liquid has evaporated.

2. Stir in the garlic, herbs, and broth or wine and cook for a couple of minutes. Stir in the tomato paste. Gradually add the spinach, turning it in the hot sauce until wilted. Season to taste with salt and pepper.

3. Melt the remaining dairy-free spread in a saucepan, add the flour, and cook for 1 minute. Gradually blend in the milk, stirring well to remove any lumps. Cook for 3-4 minutes, until thickened. Stir in the nutritional yeast, if using, or season with salt and pepper.

4. To assemble, spoon one-quarter of the mushroom sauce into a wide ovenproof dish and level. Arrange a single layer of lasagna noodles on top, snapping the sheets to fit where necessary. Drizzle with about one-third of the white sauce. Spoon another quarter of the mushroom sauce into the dish and arrange more lasagna noodles on top.

5. Repeat with another layer of mushroom sauce and lasagna noodles, then spread with the remaining mushroom sauce. Spoon the rest of the white sauce on top and sprinkle with the cheese.

6. Bake in a preheated oven, at 350°F, for 50-60 minutes, until the surface is bubbling and golden. Let stand for 10 minutes before serving.

¼ cup dairy-free spread
2 onions, chopped
2 celery stalks, chopped
9 cup coarsely chopped mushrooms (about 1¼ lb)
3 garlic cloves, crushed
2 teaspoons dried thyme or oregano
⅔ cup vegetable broth (see page 219) or vegan red wine
3 tablespoons tomato paste
1 lb fresh spinach, washed and dried
¼ cup all-purpose flour
2½ cups almond milk
3 tablespoons nutritional yeast (optional)
8 oz oven-ready lasagna noodles
1 cup shredded cheddar-style vegan cheese
salt and pepper

Serves **4-5**
Prep time **35 minutes**
Cooking time **1 hour 20 minutes**

AFFORDABILITY 2

VEGAN *Moussaka*

2 medium eggplants, cut into
 ¼ inch thick slices
¼ cup olive oil
4 Yukon Gold potatoes (about 1 lb),
 peeled and cut into ¼ inch slices
2 red onions, chopped
4 garlic cloves, crushed
⅔ cup vegetable broth (see
 page 219) or vegan red wine
7 oz plain, olive, or basil tofu
1 teaspoon dried oregano
 or thyme
1 teaspoon ground cinnamon
2 tablespoons tomato paste
2 tablespoons dairy-free spread
3 tablespoons all-purpose flour
2 cups almond milk
3 tablespoons nutritional yeast
 (optional)
salt and pepper

Serves **4**
Prep time **10 minutes**
Cooking time **1 hour**

1 Put the eggplant slices onto an aluminum foil-lined broiler rack or baking sheet and brush with 2 tablespoons of the oil. Season with salt and pepper and cook under a moderate broiler for 10 minutes, until golden. Turn the slices over and cook for another 10 minutes.

2 Meanwhile, cook the potatoes in boiling, lightly salted water for 5 minutes, and drain.

3 Heat the remaining oil in a skillet and sauté the onions for 5 minutes to soften. Add the garlic and cook for another 1 minute. Add the broth or wine and let simmer for a couple of minutes. Crumble in the tofu, then add the oregano or thyme, cinnamon, and tomato paste. Cook for 2 minutes, stirring to combine the ingredients.

4 Melt the dairy-free spread in the rinsed-out saucepan, add the flour, and cook for 1 minute. Gradually blend in the milk, stirring well to remove any lumps. Cook for 1–2 minutes, until thickened. Stir in the nutritional yeast, if using, or season with salt and pepper.

5 To assemble, spread half the tofu mixture in a shallow ovenproof dish and arrange half the potatoes and eggplant slices on top. Spoon about one-third of the sauce on top. Add the remaining tofu mixture, potatoes, and finally the eggplants. Spread with the rest of the sauce. Bake in a preheated oven, at 375°F, for 45 minutes. Serve with a leafy green salad.

SWEET POTATO, PEPPER & COCONUT *Gratin*

1. Combine the red romano peppers, onion, garlic, and chili and sprinkle about two-thirds of the mixture over the bottom of a shallow baking dish.

2. Place the potato slices vertically into the dish over the romano pepper mixture. Once all the potato slices are packed into the dish, sprinkle the remaining romano pepper mixture around them.

3. Put the peanut butter and coconut milk into a small saucepan and heat gently until the peanut butter softens enough to combine smoothly with the coconut milk. Pour it over the potatoes and cover the dish with aluminum foil.

4. Bake in a preheated oven, at 375°F, for 30 minutes. Uncover the dish and bake for another 50-60 minutes, until the potatoes are soft when pierced with a knife and the surface is turning golden.

2 red romano sweet peppers, cored, seeded, and finely chopped
1 red onion, finely chopped
3 garlic cloves, finely chopped
1 red chili, seeded and finely chopped
6 sweet potatoes (about 2 lb), scrubbed and thinly sliced
⅓ cup chunky peanut butter
1⅔ cups coconut milk

Serves **4**
Prep time **25 minutes**
Cooking time **1½ hours**

MUSHROOM
STROGANOFF

5 tablespoons olive oil
1 lb mixed mushrooms, such as
  cremini, chanterelle, shiitake,
  and button, trimmed and halved
  or quartered, if large
1 garlic clove, thinly sliced
1 large red onion, halved and
  thinly sliced
1 teaspoon whole-grain mustard
½ teaspoon English mustard
½ teaspoon ground paprika
2 tablespoons cashew butter
1 cup soy cream
¼ cup chopped flat leaf parsley
salt and pepper

Serves **4**
Prep time **15 minutes**
Cooking time **10 minutes**

1 Heat the oil in a large, heavy skillet, add the mushrooms, garlic, and onion, and cook over high heat, stirring occasionally, for 5 minutes, until golden and softened.

2 Add the mustards and paprika and continue to cook, stirring and tossing constantly, for 1–2 minutes.

3 Stir in the cashew butter and soy cream and gently heat for 1 minute, until piping hot but not boiling, otherwise the cream may separate.

4 Stir in the chopped parsley and season with a little salt and plenty of pepper. Serve on a bed of rice.

VARIATION
For vegetable stroganoff, heat 3 tablespoons of olive oil in a large, heavy skillet, add 1 large onion, thinly sliced, 2 sweet potatoes, peeled and cubed, and 1 red bell pepper, cored, seeded, and cubed, and cook over medium heat, stirring occasionally, for 5 minutes, until the onion is softened but not browned. Add ⅓ cup of water and stir again. Cover and simmer gently for 5 minutes or until the sweet potato is tender. Add ½ teaspoon of ground paprika and toss again, then stir in 1 cup cashew cream and ¼ cup of chopped flat leaf parsley and heat for 1–2 minutes over gentle heat until piping hot but not boiling, otherwise the cream may separate. Season well with salt and pepper and serve on a bed of rice.

HASH BROWN
WITH EGGPLANTS & RED ONIONS

6 Yukon Gold potatoes
(about 1½ lb)
¼ cup olive oil
2 teaspoons finely chopped
rosemary
3 red onions, sliced
1 large eggplant, cut into
¾ inch dice
2 garlic cloves, crushed
1⅓ cups shredded pizza-style
vegan cheese
12 pitted black olives
3 tablespoons capers
salt and pepper

Serves **4-6**
Prep time **30 minutes**
Cooking time **40 minutes**

1 Line a 14 × 10 inch jellyroll pan or similar size baking pan
with a rectangle of parchment paper that goes up the sides.

2 Coarsely grate the potatoes onto several layers of paper
towels. Spread out the potatoes in a thin layer and place
more layers of paper towels on top. Press the paper down
firmly to squeeze out the juice from the potatoes.

3 Transfer the potatoes to a bowl and add 2 tablespoons of
the oil, the rosemary, plenty of pepper, and a little salt.
Transfer to the pan and spread to the edges in an even
layer. Pack down firmly with the back of a large spoon.
Bake in a preheated oven, at 400°F, for 30 minutes or
until golden and cooked through.

4 While the potatoes are baking, heat the remaining oil in
a skillet and sauté the onions and eggplant for 10 minutes
or until softened and golden. Stir in the garlic for another
1 minute.

5 Transfer the vegetables onto the potato layer, spreading
them out evenly. Sprinkle with the cheese, then with the
olives and capers. Return to the oven for 10 minutes to
melt the cheese.

6 Cut into squares and transfer to serving plates with
a spatula. Serve with a salad of peppery greens.

TOMATO & THYME *Tart*

1 Put the flour into a bowl and season with salt and pepper. Add the spread and rub in with your fingertips until the mixture resembles fine bread crumbs. Stir in half the thyme, then add enough of the measured water to bring the mixture together into a firm dough.

2 Roll out the dough on a lightly floured surface and use to line a 9 inch fluted tart pan. Chill until ready to use.

3 Heat 1 tablespoon of the oil in a skillet, add the onion, and cook over medium-high heat for 5-6 minutes, until softened and golden. Stir in the remaining thyme leaves and cook for another 1 minute. Spoon the onion mixture into the pastry shell and smooth over.

4 Toss the tomatoes in a bowl with the remaining oil, salt flakes, and plenty of pepper. Arrange on top of the onion in the pastry shell and bake in a preheated oven, at 425°F, for 20-25 minutes, until the pastry is golden and the tomatoes softened and lightly charred in places. Garnish with thyme leaves to serve.

2 cups all-purpose flour, plus extra
   for dusting
½ cup dairy-free spread, cubed
¼ cup thyme leaves, plus extra
   to garnish
2-3 tablespoons cold water
3 tablespoons olive oil
1 onion, finely chopped
18 cherry tomatoes (in a mixture
   of colors), halved
½ teaspoon sea salt flakes
salt and pepper

Serves **6**
Prep time **20 minutes,**
   plus chilling
Cooking time **35 minutes**

AFFORDABILITY 1

CHICKPEA, CARROT & PRUNE *Pockets*

1 (15 oz) can chickpeas
  (garbanzo beans)
3 tablespoons olive oil
1 large onion, chopped
2 cups diced carrots
2 garlic cloves, crushed
2 teaspoons ras el hanout
  spice mix
1 teaspoon ground turmeric
12 pitted prunes, coarsely chopped
3 tablespoons chopped cilantro
salt and pepper

Basic dough

2²/₃ cups all-purpose flour
¾ cup dairy-free spread, chilled
¼ cup water
oat or rice milk, to glaze
sea salt, to sprinkle

Makes **6**
Prep time **25 minutes,
  plus cooling**
Cooking time **50 minutes**

1 To make the dough, put the flour into a bowl with a little salt and pepper. Add the dairy-free spread to the bowl, a little at a time, dusting with flour from the bowl each time so that the spread doesn't clump together. Once all the spread has been added to the flour, add the measured water and mix with a blunt knife until the mixture starts to form a dough. Add a dash more water if the mixture is still dry.

2 Turn out onto the surface and lightly knead into a ball of dough. Wrap and chill for at least 1 hour.

3 For the filling, drain the chickpeas, reserving the liquid. Break up the chickpeas by mashing them against the side of the bowl with a fork. Heat the oil in a skillet and sauté the onion and carrots for 10 minutes, stirring frequently. Add the garlic, spice mix, and turmeric and cook for another 1 minute. Remove from the heat and stir in the chickpeas, reserved chickpea liquid, prunes, and cilantro. Season to taste with salt and pepper.

4 Line a large baking sheet with parchment paper. Divide the dough into 6 even pieces and roll out each on a floured surface to a circle measuring about 7 inches in diameter. Spoon the filling onto the dough pieces, slightly to one side of the center. Fold the dough over to enclose the filling and press the edges firmly together to seal. Press and crimp the edges of the dough to seal, and transfer to the baking sheet. Brush with milk and sprinkle with sea salt.

5 Bake for about 40 minutes in a preheated oven, at 400°F, until the pastry is firm and just beginning to brown. Serve warm or cold.

Chestnut & VEGGIE GRATIN

1. Cover the dried chestnuts with the broth and soak overnight, or boil them in the broth for 1 hour.

2. Place both types of potatoes into a saucepan of water, bring to a boil, and simmer for about 25 minutes, until soft.

3. Meanwhile, heat the olive oil in a saucepan and add the tomatoes, the remaining vegetables, dates, yeast extract, and rosemary. Add the chestnuts and any remaining soaking liquid to this mixture and simmer for 15-20 minutes.

4. Drain the potatoes and mash them with the soy milk. Stir in the parsley, plus some salt and pepper.

5. Put the cornstarch and carob into a small bowl, add the vinegar, molasses, tomato paste, and orange juice, and mix into a paste. Add the paste to the chestnut mixture, then stir over low heat until the liquid thickens.

6. Divide the chestnut mixture equally among 6 (5 inch) individual ovenproof dishes. Place a layer of mashed potato on top. Bake in a preheated oven, at 350°F, for about 20 minutes, until lightly browned.

10 dried chestnuts
5 cups vegetable broth (see page 219)
6 Yukon Gold potatoes (about 1½ lb), chopped
1 sweet potato, chopped
1 tablespoon olive oil
6 tomatoes, chopped
2 onions, chopped
1 carrot, chopped
1 cup chopped cauliflower
¾ cup frozen peas
1 green bell pepper, cored, seeded, and chopped
1 small zucchini, chopped
1 tablespoon chopped dates
1 tablespoon yeast extract
6 sprigs of rosemary, leaves finely chopped
3 tablespoons sweetened soy milk
1 tablespoon chopped parsley
1 heaped tablespoon cornstarch
1 teaspoon carob powder
1 tablespoon balsamic vinegar
1 teaspoon blackstrap molasses
2 teaspoons tomato paste
4 teaspoons orange juice
salt and pepper

Serves **6**
Prep time **20 minutes**
Cooking time **45 minutes, plus soaking**

AFFORDABILITY
3

POTATO, ROSEMARY & ONION POT PIE

½ cup olive oil
1 large Spanish onion, halved and thinly sliced
8 Yukon Gold potatoes (about 2 lb), scrubbed and thinly sliced
⅓ cup chopped rosemary leaves
½ teaspoon dried chili flakes
½ teaspoon ground cumin
½ teaspoon ground coriander
⅔ cup vegetable broth (see page 219)
1 package (1 lb) ready-to-bake vegan puff pastry
all-purpose flour, for dusting
2 tablespoons soy milk
salt and pepper

Serves **4**
Prep time **30 minutes**
Cooking time **about 45 minutes**

1 Heat half the oil in a skillet, add the onion, and cook over medium-high heat for 5 minutes, until softened and beginning to turn golden. Remove and set aside.

2 Heat the remaining oil in the pan, add the potato slices, rosemary, and spices and cook, tossing and stirring frequently, for 10 minutes, until softened and lightly golden.

3 Layer the potato slices in a pie plate with the onions. Pour the broth over the slices, and season with salt and pepper.

4 Roll out the dough on a lightly floured surface to about ¾ inch wider than the top of the pie plate. Cut a thin strip of dough and place it around the edge of the dish, pressing down with a little water to seal. Lightly brush the top of the strip with water, top with the dough lid, and press around the edges with a fork to seal. Make an incision in the center of the pie for the steam to escape and lightly brush all over with the soy milk.

5 Bake in a preheated oven, at 425°F, for 25–30 minutes, until the pastry is golden and the potatoes are tender. Serve hot.

AFFORDABILITY 1

POTATO & MUSHROOM
POT PIE

3 tablespoons vegetable oil
1 lb cremini mushrooms, halved,
  or quartered if large
2 onions, thinly sliced
2 carrots, diced
3 garlic cloves, crushed
2 tablespoons all-purpose flour
1½ cups apple cider, apple juice, or
  vegan ale
1 cup water
2 teaspoons vegan bouillon powder
2 teaspoons vegan Dijon mustard
1 teaspoon dried mixed herbs
4 russet potatoes (about 1 lb),
  cut into small chunks

Basic dough
1⅔ cups all-purpose flour
1½ teaspoons baking powder
½ cup dairy-free spread, chilled
3 tablespoons water
oat or rice milk, to glaze
salt and pepper
sea salt, to sprinkle

Serves **4**
Prep time **30 minutes,**
  plus chilling and cooling
Cooking time **1 hour 10 minutes**

1 To make the dough, mix the flour and baking powder in a bowl with a little salt and pepper. Add the dairy-free spread to the bowl, a little at a time, dusting with flour from the bowl each time so that the spread doesn't clump together. Once all the spread has been added, add the measured water and mix with a blunt knife until the mixture starts to form a dough. Turn out onto the surface and lightly knead into a ball of dough. Wrap and chill for at least 1 hour.

2 Heat 1 tablespoon of the oil in a large saucepan and gently sauté the mushrooms, stirring them frequently for about 10 minutes, until all the juices have evaporated and the mushrooms are browned. Transfer to a plate.

3 Add the remaining oil to the pan with the onions and carrots and sauté for another 10 minutes. Stir in the garlic and flour and cook, stirring, for 1 minute. Gradually blend in the apple cider, apple juice, or ale and the measured water.

4 Add the bouillon powder, mustard, herbs, and potatoes and bring to a gentle simmer. Cook for about 10 minutes, until the potatoes are beginning to soften. Turn into a pie plate, piling the vegetables up in the center. Let cool.

5 Brush the edges of the pie plate with water. Roll out the dough on a lightly floured surface and position over the pie. Tidy the edges and make a hole in the center of the pie. Brush with the milk and sprinkle with sea salt. Bake in a preheated oven, at 400°F, for 35–40 minutes, until the pastry is golden. Serve hot with green vegetables.

CAULIFLOWER,
POTATO & LENTIL
Casserole

1 Melt 2 tablespoons of the dairy-free spread in a large saucepan and gently sauté the onion, leek, carrots, and celery for 5 minutes. Pour in the milk and bring to a gentle simmer. Add the lentils and bouillon powder, cover, and cook gently for 30 minutes, until the lentils are tender and the milk has thickened. Stir in the chestnuts and parsley and season to taste with salt and pepper. Transfer to a shallow pie plate.

2 Cook the potatoes in a large saucepan of boiling water for 8 minutes. Add the cauliflower and cook for another 8-10 minutes or until the vegetables are tender. Drain thoroughly, return to the pan, and mash well.

3 Add the remaining dairy-free spread and mustard to the mashed vegetables and season to taste with salt and pepper. Spoon them over the filling and spread in an even layer. Bake in a preheated oven, at 375°F, for 40-50 minutes, until crisped and pale golden. Serve with a seasonal green vegetable.

¼ cup dairy-free spread
1 onion, chopped
1 leek, trimmed and sliced
2 carrots, sliced
2 celery stalks, sliced
2½ cups almond or oat milk
1 cup French green lentils, rinsed
1 tablespoon vegan bouillon powder
12 cooked, peeled chestnuts
3 tablespoons chopped parsley
6 russet potatoes (about 1½ lb), cut into chunks
1 medium cauliflower, cut into chunks
2 tablespoons grainy mustard
salt and pepper

Serves **4**
Prep time **25 minutes**
Cooking time **1½ hours**

AFFORDABILITY
2

RATATOUILLE
with mashed parsnips

⅓ cup olive oil
1 red bell pepper, cored, seeded, and cut into chunks
1 green bell pepper, cored, seeded, and cut into chunks
1 yellow bell pepper, cored, seeded, and cut into chunks
1 garlic clove, thinly sliced
1 large eggplant, trimmed and cut into chunks
2 zucchini, trimmed and cut into chunks
5 tomatoes, coarsely chopped
⅔ cup vegetable broth (see page 219) or vegan red wine
⅔ cup water
1 vegan bouillon cube
10 parsnips (about 2½ lb), peeled and chopped
2 tablespoons soy spread
1 tablespoon chopped thyme leaves
salt and pepper

Serves **6**
Prep time **25 minutes**
Cooking time **45 minutes**

AFFORDABILITY
3

1 Heat the oil in a large, heavy skillet, add the bell peppers, garlic, eggplant, and zucchini and cook over medium-high heat, stirring and tossing occasionally, for 10 minutes, until softened and lightly golden in places. Add the tomatoes and cook for 3 minutes. Pour in the broth or wine and the measured water and bring to a boil, then cover and simmer for another 10 minutes.

2 Meanwhile, bring a large saucepan of lightly salted water to a boil, crumble in the bouillon cube with the parsnips, and mix well. Bring to a gentle simmer and cook for 10-15 minutes, until the parsnips are tender. Drain well, return to the pan, and mash with the soy spread, then stir in the thyme leaves.

3 Transfer the ratatouille mixture to a large ovenproof dish. Spoon the mashed parsnips over the vegetables and season generously with pepper. Bake in a preheated oven, at 400°F, for 20 minutes, until the top is lightly golden in places. Serve with a simple green salad.

VARIATION
For roasted vegetables & parsnips, cut 3 different-colored bell peppers into chunks, then put into a large roasting pan along with 2 zucchini, trimmed and cut into chunks, and 2 parsnips, peeled and cut into chunks. Drizzle with ¼ cup of olive oil, sprinkle with 2 tablespoons of chopped rosemary, and season with salt and pepper. Roast in a preheated oven, at 400°F, for 20 minutes, until soft and lightly golden in places. Add 4 tomatoes, cut into chunks, to the pan and gently toss, then roast for another 10 minutes. Serve hot in warm serving bowls with crusty bread to mop up the juices.

POTATO & PEPPER
SALTADO

1. Cook the potatoes in boiling, lightly salted water for about 3 minutes, until slightly softened but keeping their shape. Drain thoroughly in a strainer and pat dry between several sheets of paper towels.

2. Put the cornstarch into a small bowl and gradually blend in the measured water. Add the coriander, dried herbs, soy sauce, vinegar, mustard, and sugar. Mix well.

3. Heat 2 tablespoons of the oil in a skillet and add the potatoes. Cook gently for about 10 minutes, turning the potatoes frequently, until golden brown and cooked through. Drain the potatoes onto a plate. Add the nuts to the pan and cook briefly until lightly browned. Add to the plate with the potatoes.

4. Add the remaining oil to the skillet with the bell peppers and onions and sauté gently for 10-12 minutes, until both onion and bell peppers are beginning to brown. Stir in the spice mixture and cook for 1 minute, stirring until the juices start to thicken.

5. Add the potatoes and nuts and heat briefly to warm through. Transfer to serving plates and sprinkle with parsley to serve.

1 lb new potatoes, scrubbed and cut into small sticks
1 teaspoon cornstarch
⅓ cup water
1 teaspoon ground coriander
1 teaspoon mixed dried herbs
½ teaspoon dried mint
4 teaspoons soy sauce
2 teaspoons vegan red or white wine vinegar
1 teaspoon vegan Dijon mustard
2 teaspoons packed light brown sugar
3 tablespoons vegetable oil or mild olive oil
3 tablespoons blanched almonds or cashew nuts, coarsely chopped
1 green bell pepper, cored, seeded, and sliced
1 red bell pepper, cored, seeded, and sliced
1 yellow bell pepper, cored, seeded, and sliced
2 red onions, sliced
small handful of parsley, stems removed and leaves finely chopped

Serves **2**
Prep time **20 minutes**
Cooking time **30 minutes**

AFFORDABILITY
2

BATTERED VEGGIES
with Mashed Peas

1. Cut the carrots and parsnips lengthwise into thin wedges. Halve the onion and cut each half into 4 wedges so the root end keeps the wedges intact. Bring a saucepan of water to a boil and cook the vegetables for 2 minutes to soften slightly. Drain thoroughly.

2. Cook the peas in boiling water for 3 minutes. Drain, return to the pan, and mash well using a potato masher. Beat in the mint, dairy-free spread, and ¼ cup of boiling water.

3. For the batter, put the flour, baking powder, and bouillon powder into a bowl. Make a well in the center of the bowl and pour in half the apple cider, apple juice, or beer. Beat with a wire balloon whisk to make a smooth thick batter. Gradually whisk in the remaining liquid.

4. Sprinkle a little flour onto a large plate, add the carrots, parsnips, and onions, and turn in the flour to coat.

5. Pour a 1 inch depth of oil into a large saucepan or deep skillet and heat until a teaspoon of the batter sizzles on the surface. Add some of the vegetables to the batter, turning them until coated. Lift out and carefully lower into the oil using a slotted spoon. Fry for 3–4 minutes, until the batter is crisp and turning pale golden. Lift out with the slotted spoon onto a plate lined with paper towels. Cook the remaining vegetables in the same way. Reheat the mashed peas and serve with the battered veggies.

4 carrots (about 8 oz)
2 parsnips (about 8 oz)
1 onion
1 ⅓ cups frozen peas
2 teaspoons finely chopped mint
1 tablespoon dairy-free spread
¾ cup all-purpose flour, plus extra for dusting
1 teaspoon baking powder
1 teaspoon vegan bouillon powder
1 cup apple cider, apple juice, or vegan beer
vegetable oil, for frying
salt and pepper

Serves **2**
Prep time **25 minutes**
Cooking time **20 minutes**

AFFORDABILITY

VEGAN DINNER PARTY

Whether your friends are vegan or they love nothing more than enjoying a T-bone, you can still gather everyone around the dining table for a fabulous meat-free dinner. It's a good opportunity to showcase some interesting vegan recipes, and to introduce your pals to ingredients and creative combinations that they might not have encountered before.

Of course, a successful dinner party isn't all about the food—you will need to invite friends who will probably get along. It's also important to check you've got enough chairs, dinnerware, and cutlery for the number of people you're expecting. Eating dinner with a spoon instead of a fork, or sitting cross-legged on the living room floor with a plate of spaghetti, isn't everyone's idea of a relaxing evening.

PLAN AHEAD

Once you've chosen your menu, check the cupboards and make a shopping list. It's a good idea to check with your friends to be sure that no one has an allergy or really doesn't like a particular ingredient. You should also double-check that everyone knows it's a vegan meal—people often bring items for the meal or as a thank you gift, and your guests will be embarrassed if they turn up with nonvegan offerings.

On the day, get yourself prepared well ahead of your guests' arrival. Prepping and cooking food often takes longer than you estimate, especially if you're cooking something new. It's also good to get all the peeling, chopping, and mixing out of the way so that you can relax and talk to your friends instead of spend the entire evening in the kitchen. If you haven't hosted a dinner party before, the trick is to prepare a cold appetizer and a cold dessert ahead of time, and keep them in the refrigerator. Alternatively, just serve plates of cold nibbles and dips as an appetizer, leaving you to concentrate on the main dish.

LAID-BACK DINNER WITH FRIENDS

Appetizer: Tapenade Bruschetta (see page 42)

Main: Farro Burgers with Oven Fries (see page 163)

Dessert: Chocolate Mousse Cakes with Summer Berries (see page 206)

ROMANTIC MEAL FOR TWO

Appetizer: Chilled Gazpacho (see page 35)

Main: Pea & Mint Pesto Fettuccine (see page 104)

Dessert: Ultrarich Chocolate Stacks (see page 200)

TV NIGHT-ON-THE-COUCH DINNER

Appetizer: Hot & Smoky Hummus (see page 88)

Main: Vegan Moussaka (see page 144)

Dessert: Raspberry, Pistachio & Rose Semifreddo (see page 211)

THAI CHICKPEA BURGERS

1 Pulse together the scallions, lemongrass, ginger, chili, garlic, and cilantro in a food processor until finely chopped. Add the chickpeas, then pulse again until coarsely blended.

2 Add the flour and season with salt and pepper, then process until the mixture forms a coarse thick paste. Shape the mixture into 4 patties.

3 Heat the oil in a skillet, add the patties, and cook on each side for 2-3 minutes, until browned. Serve with a bean sprout and bell pepper salad, if you want.

VARIATION

For Mexican bean burgers, pulse together 4 scallions, 1 garlic clove, a handful of cilantro leaves, and 1 teaspoon each of chili powder, ground cumin, and ground coriander in a food processor. Add 2 cups rinsed and drained, mixed canned beans, such as kidney beans, black beans, and pinto beans, and pulse again until coarsely blended. Add 2 tablespoons of whole-wheat flour and 3 tablespoons of plain soy yogurt and season with salt and pepper. Blend until the mixture forms a coarse thick paste. Shape into 4 patties and cook as above. Serve in vegan buns with guacamole and tomato salsa.

4 scallions
1 lemongrass stalk, outer leaves removed
¾ inch piece of fresh ginger root, peeled and chopped
1 red chili, halved and seeded
1 garlic clove, peeled
handful of cilantro leaves
1 (15 oz) can chickpeas (garbanzo beans), drained and rinsed
2 tablespoons whole-wheat flour
3 tablespoons canola oil
salt and pepper

Serves **4**
Prep time **20 minutes**
Cooking time **10 minutes**

AFFORDABILITY

FARRO BURGERS
with oven fries

1 Put the farro and broth into a saucepan and bring to a simmer. Cook gently for about 15 minutes, until the farro is soft and most of the broth has been absorbed. Drain thoroughly through a strainer.

2 Cut the potatoes into chunky sticks, then toss with 1 tablespoon of the oil and plenty of salt and pepper. Spread out on a baking sheet and bake in a preheated oven, at 425°F, for 35-40 minutes, until golden. Turn the potatoes once or twice with a spatula during cooking.

3 Heat another 1 tablespoon of the oil in a skillet and sauté the onion for 5 minutes. Add the carrots and cook for another 5 minutes. Once cooled, transfer to a food processor with the pickles, herbs, almond butter, farro, and plenty of black pepper, then blend until the ingredients cling together but retain a little texture.

4 Turn out onto the work surface and shape into a compact cake. Cut into 8 even wedges. Shape each into a compact ball and flatten firmly into patty shapes.

5 Heat the remaining oil in the skillet and gently cook the cakes for about 3 minutes, until golden on the underside. Carefully turn over with a spatula and cook for another 2 minutes. Serve with the oven fries, vegan mayonnaise, and tomato salad.

¾ cup farro, soaked in water overnight and rinsed
2 cups vegetable broth (see page 219)
9 Yukon Gold potatoes (about 2 lb 4 oz), scrubbed
¼ cup mild olive oil or vegetable oil
1 large onion, chopped
2¾ cups shredded carrots
⅓ cup chopped pickles
3 tablespoons chopped dill, tarragon or parsley
2 tablespoons almond butter
salt and pepper

To serve
vegan mayonnaise or Soynnaise (see page 218)
tomato salad

Serves **4**
Prep time **20 minutes**
Cooking time **1 hour 10 minutes**

TOFU & CARAMELIZED ONION
SAUSAGES
with Cauliflower puree

¼ cup mild olive oil
3 red onions, chopped
1 teaspoon sugar
2 teaspoons chopped thyme
1 garlic clove, chopped
2 slices vegan white or
  whole-wheat bread
7 oz plain or olive-flavored tofu
1 small cauliflower, cut into
  small florets
2 teaspoons cornstarch
1½ teaspoons vegan bouillon
  powder
1 teaspoon balsamic vinegar
salt and pepper

Serves **2-3**
Prep time **30 minutes**
Cooking time **25 minutes**

AFFORDABILITY
1

1 Heat 2 tablespoons of the oil in a skillet and add the onions and sugar. Sauté gently, stirring frequently, until they are deep golden and tender, about 10 minutes. Transfer half to a plate and add the thyme and garlic to the pan. Sauté for another 1 minute.

2 Tear the bread into small pieces and put into a food processor or blender. Blend to make coarse bread crumbs. Add the onion, thyme, and garlic mixture and crumble in the tofu. Blend until the mixture is fine enough to hold together when a small amount is pressed into a ball.

3 Transfer to the work surface and compact the mixture into a cake. Cut into 6 wedges and shape each into a sausage.

4 Cook the cauliflower in boiling water for 8 minutes or until tender. Drain through a colander, reserving the liquid. Puree about two-thirds of the cauliflower and a dash of the cooking liquid in a food processor or high-speed blender until smooth. Season with salt and pepper and return the puree to the saucepan with the remaining cauliflower florets.

5 Heat the remaining oil in the skillet and cook the sausages for 5 minutes, turning frequently until browned. Lift out and keep warm.

6 Blend the cornstarch with a dash of water and make up to 1¼ cups with the cauliflower cooking liquid. Add to the pan with the reserved onions and the bouillon powder. Bring to a boil, stirring until thickened. Stir in the vinegar and season to taste. Gently reheat the cauliflower puree and serve with the tofu sausages and gravy.

WALNUT & APPLE LOAF

AFFORDABILITY
1

1. Line a small loaf pan with a capacity of about 4 cups with parchment paper, pushing the paper into the corners.

2. Heat the oil in a skillet and sauté the fennel for 5 minutes. Add the walnuts and garlic and cook for another 2 minutes.

3. Put the bread in a food processor and blend to make fresh coarse crumbs. Add the walnut mixture and blend until the nuts are finely chopped. Peel, core, and grate the apple into the mixture. Add the cilantro, paprika, sugar, and a little salt and blend briefly to mix.

4. Pack firmly into the pan and level the surface. Bake in a preheated oven, at 350°F, for 30 minutes. Lift out of the pan, peel away the sides of the paper, and return to the oven for another 10 minutes. Let stand for 10 minutes.

5. In a small bowl, combine the ketchup and balsamic vinegar. Thickly slice the nut loaf and serve with the sauce.

3 tablespoons olive oil
1 large fennel bulb, chopped
2 cups walnut pieces
3 garlic cloves, chopped
3 slices vegan white or whole-wheat bread, torn into pieces
1 crisp, sweet apple
1/3 cup chopped cilantro
1 teaspoon ground paprika
2 teaspoons sugar
1/4 cup ketchup
2 tablespoons balsamic vinegar
salt and pepper

Serves **4**
Prep time **20 minutes**
Cooking time **50 minutes**

LET'S BAKE

DATE & PRUNE BROWNIES

ALMOND, RASPBERRY
& DATE BARS

PLUM, BANANA
& APPLE CRISPS

HERB & WALNUT RYE SODA BREAD

Chili & Zucchini FOCACCIA

1. Sift the flour into a bowl. Add the yeast to one side and the salt to the other side. Add 2 tablespoons of the oil and the measured water and mix to form a dough, adding a little more water if the dough seems dry.

2. Turn out the dough onto a lightly floured surface and knead for 10 minutes, until smooth and stretchy. Put the dough into a clean bowl, cover with plastic wrap, and let rise in a warm place for about 1 hour, until doubled in size.

3. Turn out the dough onto a lightly floured surface and knead lightly for 1 minute. Press or roll the dough into a coarsely shaped rectangle about 1/2 inch thick and place on a lightly oiled baking sheet. Loosely cover and let prove for 20 minutes.

4. Meanwhile, heat 1 tablespoon of the remaining oil in a skillet, add the onion, and cook over medium heat for about 3 minutes, until just softened. Add the zucchini and chili and cook for another 3 minutes. Set aside.

5. Use your fingertips to make indentations into the dough's surface. Drizzle the remaining oil over the dough and bake in a preheated oven, at 400°F, for 10 minutes. Sprinkle with the vegetable mixture, salt flakes, and rosemary sprigs, then bake for another 10-15 minutes, until golden. Let cool on a wire rack.

3²/₃ cups white bread flour, plus extra for dusting
2¼ teaspoons active dry yeast
1 teaspoon salt
¼ cup olive oil, plus extra for oiling
1 cup plus 2 tablespoons warm water
½ small onion, thinly sliced
½ small zucchini, trimmed and thinly sliced
1 red chili, seeded and thinly sliced
1 teaspoon sea salt flakes
few small rosemary sprigs

Serves **6**
Prep time **30 minutes, plus proving**
Cooking time **30-35 minutes**

AFFORDABILITY 1

Toasted
POTATO BREAD
WITH TOMATOES

3 russet potatoes (about 12 oz),
  peeled and cut into chunks
1 teaspoon active dry yeast
1 teaspoon sugar
1 tablespoon sunflower oil,
  plus extra for oiling
1½ cups white bread flour,
  plus extra for dusting
¾ cup whole-wheat bread flour
2 tablespoons chopped rosemary
1 tablespoon thyme leaves
salt and pepper

Topping
2 tablespoons olive oil
18 cherry tomatoes (in a mixture
  of colors), halved
½ teaspoon thyme leaves
½ teaspoon sea salt flakes

Serves **4**
Prep time **30 minutes,**
  plus proving and cooling
Cooking time **1 hour**

1 Cook the potato chunks in a large saucepan of lightly salted boiling water for 15-20 minutes, until tender but not mushy. Drain really well, reserving the cooking liquid.

2 Put ⅓ cup of the cooking liquid into a large bowl and let cool until lukewarm. Sprinkle the yeast over the water, then stir in the sugar and set aside for 10 minutes.

3 Mash the potatoes with the oil, then stir in the yeast mixture and mix well with a wooden spoon. Mix in the flours, herbs, and salt and pepper, then turn out onto a lightly floured surface and knead well to incorporate the last of the flour. Knead the dough until soft and pliable, then put into a lightly oiled bowl, cover with plastic wrap, and let rise in a warm place for 1 hour, until well risen.

4 Knead the dough on a lightly floured surface, then coarsely shape it into a round, place on a baking sheet, and lightly cover it with oiled plastic wrap. Let prove in a warm place for 30 minutes. Score an X into the top of the dough with a sharp knife and bake in a preheated oven, at 425°F, for 35-40 minutes, until well risen and crusty on top. Transfer to a wire rack to cool for 30 minutes.

5 Cut 4 slices of the bread and lightly toast. Meanwhile, heat the oil for the topping in a skillet, add the tomatoes, and cook over high heat for 2-3 minutes, until softened. Stir in the thyme and salt flakes. Serve with the toasted bread, seasoned with pepper.

AFFORDABILITY
1

HERB & WALNUT RYE SODA BREAD

1 Mix together the flour, walnuts, mixed herbs, baking soda, xanthan gum, and salt in a large bowl, then make a well in the center. Whisk together the rice milk and canola oil in a bowl, then pour into the well and stir in with a wooden spoon until a soft, slightly sticky dough is formed.

2 Turn out the dough onto a lightly floured surface and pat into a 7 inch round. Place onto a baking sheet. Sprinkle with the extra walnuts and gently press to adhere to the dough. Make a deep X into the top of the dough with a sharp knife, then let stand in a warm place for 30 minutes.

3 Bake in a preheated oven, at 425°F, for 40-45 minutes, until the bread is crisp on the outside and cooked through; the bottom should sound hollow when tapped with your fingertips. Turn out onto a wire rack to cool before slicing thickly to serve.

VARIATION

For pumpkin & sunflower seed whole-wheat soda bread, mix together 2 cups whole-wheat flour, 1 teaspoon of baking soda, 2 teaspoons of xanthan gum, and ¼ cup each of sunflower seeds and pumpkin seeds in a large bowl. Make a well in the center. Continue with the recipe as above, adding the rice milk and canola oil to make a dough and preparing it on the baking sheet for baking. After cutting the X into the dough, sprinkle with an extra tablespoon of pumpkin seeds and let prove in a warm place for 30 minutes. Bake, cool, and serve as above.

2½ cups rye flour
⅓ cup coarsely chopped walnuts, plus 1 tablespoon coarsely chopped for sprinkling
¼ cup chopped mixed herbs, such as rosemary, parsley, or thyme
1 teaspoon baking soda
2 teaspoons xanthan gum
¼ teaspoon salt
1 cup rice milk
2 tablespoons canola oil, plus extra for oiling

Serves **6**
Preparation time **15 minutes, plus standing**
Cooking time **40-45 minutes**

AFFORDABILITY
1

Vanilla & jam SHORTBREAD

1 Beat the spread and superfine or granulated sugar together in a bowl until pale and fluffy. Sift the flour and cornstarch together into the mixture, add the vanilla, and mix until combined. Roll the dough into a ball, wrap in plastic wrap, and chill for 30 minutes.

2 Roll out the dough on a lightly floured surface to about ¼ inch thick. Use a 2 inch square or round cutter to cut out 16 squares or rounds, rerolling the scraps as necessary. Place on 2 baking sheets lined with parchment paper and bake in a preheated oven, at 325°F, for 10-12 minutes, until pale golden.

3 Let the shortbreads cool on the baking sheets for 10 minutes, until firm, then transfer to a wire rack to cool completely.

4 Sandwich the cookies together with the jam and dust with confectioners' sugar.

VARIATION

For jam & coconut streusel tarts, make the shortbread dough and chill as above. Roll out the dough as above, then use a 3 inch round cutter to cut out 12 rounds, rerolling the scraps as necessary. Use the rounds to line 12 cup of a muffin pan. Add a teaspoonful of raspberry or strawberry jam to each lined hole. Put 3 tablespoons of all-purpose flour, ⅓ cup of superfine or granulated sugar, ¼ cup of dairy-free spread, and 3 tablespoons of unsweetened dry coconut into a bowl and rub together with your fingertips until crumbly. Sprinkle the mixture over the jam and bake in a preheated oven, at 325°F, for 15 minutes, until golden.

½ cup dairy-free spread
¼ cup superfine sugar or granulated sugar
1¼ cups all-purpose flour, plus extra for dusting
3 tablespoons cornstarch
1 teaspoon vanilla extract
3 tablespoons raspberry jam or strawberry jam
confectioners' sugar, for dusting

Makes **8**
Prep time **30 minutes, plus chilling**
Cooking time **10-12 minutes**

AFFORDABILITY
1

ALMOND, RASPBERRY & DATE BARS

1   Heat the almond butter, agave syrup, margarine, and brown sugar in a saucepan over low heat, stirring constantly, until melted. Add the oats, flour, cinnamon, and dates and mix well.

2   Transfer the dough to a lightly oiled 7 × 11 inch shallow baking pan and level with the back of a metal spoon, slightly dampened to ease spreading.

3   With a teaspoon, make holes in the dough and press in the raspberries, then sprinkle with the walnuts, sesame seeds, and sunflower seeds. Bake in a preheated oven, at 375°F, for 15 minutes, or until the edges turn a pale golden brown.

4   Let cool in the pan for 10 minutes before scoring into 12 bars, then let cool completely before cutting completely into bars and carefully removing from the pan.

⅓ cup chunky almond butter
½ cup agave syrup
¼ cup soy margarine
¼ cup packed light brown sugar
2 cups rolled oats
2 tablespoons rice flour
½ teaspoon ground cinnamon
1 cup pitted and chopped fresh Medjool dates
1 cup raspberries
¼ cup coarsely chopped walnuts
1 teaspoon sesame seeds
1 tablespoon sunflower seeds
sunflower oil, for oiling

Makes **12**
Prep time **10 minutes**
Cooking time **15 minutes**

Sugar-free
FRUIT GRANOLA BARS

1 Line a baking sheet with parchment paper. Toss the apple with the lemon juice, agave syrup, and cinnamon in a bowl, then spread out on the lined baking sheet and roast in a preheated oven, at 325°F, for 20 minutes. Remove from the oven and let cool.

2 Increase the oven temperature to at 350°F. Put all the ingredients for the granola into a food processor and pulse a few times until mixed. Fold in the cooled roasted apple. Lightly oil an 8 inch square shallow cake pan with the sunflower oil, spoon in the granola mixture, and level with the back of a spoon. Bake in the oven for 20 minutes.

3 Let cool for 15 minutes before cutting into 9 squares to serve.

2 cups peeled, cored, and coarsely chopped, sweet crisp apples
1 tablespoon lemon juice
1 tablespoon agave syrup
½ teaspoon ground cinnamon
sunflower oil, for oiling

Granola
1 cup rolled oats
¾ cup dried apricots
1 cup pitted and coarsely chopped, fresh Medjool dates
2 tablespoons ground flaxseed
2 tablespoons smooth peanut butter
¼ cup agave syrup

Makes **9**
Prep time **20 minutes,**
    plus cooling
Cooking time **40 minutes**

AFFORDABILITY 2

CRANBERRY SCONES
& Compote

6 tablespoons soy milk
1 tablespoon apple cider vinegar
1 tablespoon ground golden
   flaxseed
2¼ cups all-purpose flour, plus
   extra for dusting
¼ cup granulated sugar
1 teaspoon baking powder
½ teaspoon baking soda
1 teaspoon ground cinnamon
½ cup dairy-free spread, cubed,
   plus extra for greasing
1 cup dried cranberries
1 tablespoon demera sugar or
   sugar crystals

Compote
1 cup hulled and quartered
   strawberries
2 tablespoons sugar
1 cup blackberries

Serves **6**
Prep time **20 minutes,**
   plus standing and cooling
Cooking time **25 minutes**

1 Mix ⅓ cup of the soy milk, the vinegar, and flaxseed
   together in a bowl, then let stand for 10 minutes (the
   mixture will separate slightly and thicken).

2 Meanwhile, heat the strawberries and sugar for the compote
   in a saucepan over gentle heat for 2–3 minutes, until the
   sugar dissolves. Add the blackberries and cook for another
   2–3 minutes, until the fruit softens and a juice forms.
   Remove from the heat and let cool.

3 Put the flour into a large bowl and stir in the granulated
   sugar, baking powder, baking soda, and cinnamon. Add the
   spread and rub in with your fingertips until the mixture
   resembles fine bread crumbs. Stir in the cranberries, then
   add the soy milk mixture and mix to form a soft dough.

4 Roll the dough out on a lightly floured work surface to a
   7 inch round and score into 6 wedges with a knife. Place
   on a lightly greased baking sheet, brush with the remaining
   soy milk, and sprinkle with the sugar crystals.

5 Bake in a preheated oven, at 400°F, for 15–18 minutes, until
   golden and cooked through. Let cool slightly, then serve
   warm with the cooled compote.

VARIATION
For lemon & blueberry scones, finely grate the zest of 1 lemon,
then squeeze the juice. Mix ⅓ cup of soy milk, 1 tablespoon of
ground golden flaxseed and the lemon juice together in a bowl,
then let stand for 10 minutes. Make the dough as above, stirring in
the lemon zest and 1 cup blueberries in place of the cranberries.
Roll out on a lightly floured surface to an 8 inch round and score
into 6 wedges. Place on a lightly greased baking sheet and bake
as above. Serve warm.

Peach, Apricot & Fig
CRISP

Crumb topping
1 cup whole-wheat flour
2 tablespoons canola oil
2 tablespoons sweetened soy milk
⅓ cup rolled oats
¼ cup packed dark brown sugar
¼ cup slivered almonds
2 peaches, pitted and sliced
1½ cups chopped dried apricots
6 fresh or dried figs, diced
juice of 1 lime
¼ teaspoon ground nutmeg
1 teaspoon ground cinnamon

Custard
2 tablespoons cornstarch
3 tablespoons maple syrup
2½ cups oat milk or soy milk

Serves **6**
Prep time **15 minutes**
Cooking time **30 minutes**

1 Pour the flour into a large bowl and lightly mix in the oil and soy milk with a fork until the mixture forms coarse crumbs. Stir the oats, sugar, and almonds into the mixture.

2 Put the fruit into a 1 quart ovenproof dish and sprinkle it with about ¼ cup of water, the lime juice, nutmeg, and cinnamon.

3 Spoon the crumb topping mixture over the fruit and bake in a preheated oven, at 350°F, for 25-30 minutes, until golden brown.

4 Put the cornstarch into a bowl, add the maple syrup and ¼ cup of the oat milk, and stir together well.

5 Heat the remaining milk in a small saucepan until hot but not boiling, then remove from the heat and gradually stir in the cornstarch mixture to thicken. Return the pan to a medium heat and cook for a few minutes, stirring constantly.

6 Serve the crisp with the hot custard.

PLUM, BANANA & APPLE
CRISPS

6 plums, halved and pitted
¼ cup vegan margarine
2 sweet, crisp apples, such as
  Golden Delicious, Pink Lady, or
  Pippin, peeled, cored, and cut
  into chunks
2 tablespoons demerara sugar
  or light brown sugar
2 bananas, cut into chunks
½ teaspoon ground cinnamon
pinch of ground allspice (optional)

Crumb topping
¾ cup all-purpose flour
¼ cup vegan margarine, cubed
¼ cup demerara sugar
¼ cup rolled oats

Serves **4**
Prep time **15 minutes**
Cooking time **30 minutes**

1 Cook the plums with the vegan margarine in a saucepan over gentle heat for 3 minutes. Add the apples and sugar and cook, stirring occasionally, for another 2–3 minutes.

2 Remove the pan from the heat, add the bananas and spices, and toss gently to lightly coat all the fruit in the sugar and spices. Divide the mixture among 4 (1 cup) gratin dishes.

3 Put the flour for the crumb topping into a bowl, add the margarine, and rub in with your fingertips until the mixture resembles fine bread crumbs. Stir in the sugar and oats.

4 Spoon evenly over the top of the fruit in each dish, place the dishes on a baking sheet, and bake in a preheated oven, at 400°F, for 20 minutes, until the topping is golden and the fruit is bubbling. Serve with natural soy yogurt, if you want.

AFFORDABILITY
1

Date & Prune BROWNIES

2 cups whole-wheat flour
1 cup rice milk or water
¼ cup soy milk
¼ cup canola oil
3 tablespoons unsweetened cocoa powder
1 tablespoon carob powder
1 cup packed dark brown sugar
1 teaspoon salt
1 teaspoon vanilla extract
¾ cup dried prunes, pitted
2 medjool dates, pitted
1½ teaspoons baking powder
1 tablespoon almond meal

Makes **8-10**
Prep time **15 minutes**
Cooking time **25-35 minutes**

AFFORDABILITY
1

1 Line a 10½ × 6½ × 1½ inch baking pan with parchment paper and oil lightly.

2 Put 2 heaping tablespoons of the flour into a saucepan and mix in the rice milk. Cook, stirring constantly, over medium heat until thick. Set aside to cool completely.

3 Combine the soy milk, oil, cocoa, and carob in a bowl and stir until smooth.

4 Transfer the cooled flour mixture to a food processer or liquidizer, add the sugar, salt, vanilla, prunes, and dates, and blend until smooth. Add the cocoa mixture and blend again.

5 In a bowl, mix the remaining flour with the baking powder and almond meal, then add to the prune mixture and blend again.

6 Pour the batter into the prepared pan and bake in a preheated oven, at 350°F, for 25-35 minutes, until firm to the touch.

7 Cut into slices and serve hot with a scoop of vegan ice cream and some grated dairy-free chocolate.

CHOCOLATE CHIP COOKIES

1 Line a baking sheet with parchment paper and grease with coconut oil.

2 Put the flour, sugar, cinnamon, carob powder, salt, and dates into a bowl and mix well. Add the milk, oil, and vanilla extract and beat with an electric mixer or fork. Stir in the orange zest and chocolate.

3 Place 12 spoonfuls of the dough onto the prepared baking sheet and smooth the tops with a wet knife.

4 Bake the cookies for 10 minutes in a preheated oven, at 350°F, then cool on a wire rack. Store in an airtight container until needed.

coconut oil, for greasing
1 cup whole-wheat flour or
  all-purpose flour
1 teaspoon baking powder
¼ cup packed light brown sugar
1 teaspoon ground cinnamon
4 teaspoons carob powder
pinch of salt
⅓ cup finely chopped dates
½ cup sweetened soy milk
¼ cup canola oil
1 teaspoon vanilla extract
1 teaspoon finely grated
  orange zest
3 tablespoons coarsely grated or
  chopped dairy-free chocolate
  or carob

Makes **12**
Prep time **10 minutes**
Cooking time **10 minutes**

STUDENT TIP

COMPARE PRICES Thanks to the Internet, you can now compare the price of your grocery shopping down to the last peanut. Shop with your head, not your heart, and take your money to the grocery store with the best prices.

AFFORDABILITY 1

AFFORDABILITY 1

GINGER & CHOCOLATE COOKIES

1/3 cup light corn syrup
1/4 cup dairy-free spread
1 1/2 cups rolled oats
2/3 cup whole-wheat flour or
   all-purpose flour
1 teaspoon baking powder
4 pieces well-drained preserved
   ginger in syrup, finely chopped
2 oz bittersweet dairy-free
   chocolate, coarsely chopped

Makes **14**
Prep time **20 minutes**
Cooking time **15 minutes**

1　Heat the light corn syrup and dairy-free spread in a
   small saucepan over gentle heat until melted, stirring.
   Let cool slightly.

2　Mix all the remaining ingredients together in a large bowl.
   Pour in the syrup mixture and mix to form a soft dough.
   Place 14 spoonfuls of the dough, well spaced apart, on a
   large baking sheet lined with parchment paper and gently
   press with the back of a spoon to flatten slightly.

3　Bake in a preheated oven, at 350°F, for 8–10 minutes,
   until pale golden.

4　Let the cookies cool on the baking sheet for 5 minutes,
   until firm, then transfer to a wire rack to cool completely.

STUDENT TIP

CUT YOUR COFFEE COSTS Buy a reusable coffee
cup and make your own hot beverage before leaving your
accommodations. Over the year, this can save you
a small fortune on expensive cafeteria cappuccinos
and shrink your carbon footprint.

ALL THINGS SWEET

RAW CHOCOLATE MUD PIE

CHEWY CHERRY BITES

RASPBERRY, PISTACHIO
& ROSE SEMIFREDDO

WATERMELON & LIME
GRENADINE SQUARES

CHARGRILLED FRUIT
with chili salt

1 Cut the mango into ¾ inch pieces and cut the pineapple into small wedges. Skewer the fruit onto metal or wooden skewers presoaked in water for 30 minutes, alternating the fruits.

2 Mix together the chili flakes and salt and set aside.

3 Preheat a ridged grill pan to medium heat and grill the skewers on each side for 3 minutes, until golden and caramelized. Remove the skewers from the heat, sprinkle with the salt chili mix, and serve.

1 large mango, peeled and pitted
½ pineapple, peeled
2 bananas
½ teaspoon dried chili flakes
1 tablespoon sea salt

Serves **6-8**
Prep time **15 minutes**
Cooking time **10 minutes**

STUDENT TIP

SHOP LATE Many grocery stores seriously reduce their prices on fresh produce about to pass their expiration date just before closing time. Although 24-hour trading has cut down on this to a certain extent, you can still grab a bargain if you head to the stores late in the day.

AFFORDABILITY
1

STUFFED SPICE-ROASTED PEARS

1 Halve the pears, then remove a small slice from the back of each so that they sit level in a roasting pan. Scoop out the core and seeds, leaving the stem intact.

2 Mix the prunes and hazelnuts with the cinnamon and maple syrup in a bowl, then fold in the blackberries.

3 Pile the mixture into the pear cavities and top each with a small pat of the dairy-free spread. Cover the roasting pan with aluminum foil and bake in a preheated oven, at 400°F, for 25 minutes.

4 Remove the foil and roast for another 10 minutes. Serve with the juices spooned over the pears along with a scoop of soy ice cream or soy yogurt, if you want.

VARIATION
For stuffed roasted apples with agave syrup, cut 4 apples in half and scoop out the core, leaving the stem intact. Remove a small slice from the back of each apple half so that it sits level in a roasting pan. Mix 2 coarsely chopped dried figs and ¼ cup lightly roasted almonds with ¼ cup of agave syrup in a bowl, then fold in ½ cup of raspberries. Spoon into the apple cavities and cover the pan with foil. Bake, then serve as above.

4 ripe pears
3 pitted prunes, coarsely chopped
¼ cup roasted hazelnuts,
    coarsely chopped
½ teaspoon ground cinnamon
¼ cup maple syrup
½ cup blackberries, halved
¼ cup dairy-free spread

Serves **4**
Prep time **20 minutes**
Cooking time **35 minutes**

AFFORDABILITY
1

POACHED PEACHES
& RASPBERRIES

1 Pour the measured water and apple juice or sherry into a saucepan, then add the sugar. Slit the vanilla bean lengthwise and scrape out the black seeds from inside the pod. Add these to the water with the pod, then gently heat the mixture until the sugar has dissolved.

2 Put the peach halves into an ovenproof dish so that they sit together snugly. Pour over the hot syrup, then cover and cook in a preheated oven, at 350°F, for 20 minutes.

3 Sprinkle the raspberries over the top. Serve the fruit either warm or cold. Spoon into serving bowls and decorate with the vanilla bean cut into thin strips.

1 cup water
²/₃ cup apple juice or sweet sherry
¹/₃ cup sugar
1 vanilla bean
6 peaches, halved and pitted
1 cup fresh raspberries

Serves **6**
Preparation time **15 minutes**
Cooking time **25 minutes**

AFFORDABILITY

POACHED
Pears

1¼ cups vegan red wine
1 cup water
rind and juice of 1 orange
1 cinnamon stick, broken into
  large pieces
6 cloves
2 small fresh bay leaves
⅓ cup sugar
6 pears
1 tablespoon cornstarch

Serves **6**
Prep time **10 minutes**
Cooking time **12 minutes**

1 Pour the wine and measured water into a saucepan that will hold the pears snugly. Cut the orange rind into thin strips, then add to the pan with the orange juice, spices, bay leaves, and sugar. Heat gently until the sugar has dissolved.

2 Peel the pears, leaving the stems on, then add them to the orange-flavored syrup. Simmer gently for 10 minutes, turning the pears several times so that they cook and color evenly.

3 Lift the pears out of the pan and put onto a plate. Mix the cornstarch with a little water in a cup, then stir into the flavored syrup and bring to a boil, stirring until thickened and smooth. Add the pears and let cool.

4 Transfer to shallow dishes and serve.

AFFORDABILITY
2

APRICOT & PAPAYA WHIP

150 g (5 oz) ready-to-eat dried apricots, chopped
25 g (1 oz) dried papaya, chopped
450 ml (¾ pint) sweetened soy milk
2 tablespoons flax oil
6 strawberries or 1 kiwi fruit, to decorate

Serves **6**
Prep time **5 minutes, plus soaking and chilling**

1 Soak the dried apricots and papaya in the soy milk overnight.

2 Transfer the dried fruit and soy milk to a food processor or liquidizer and blend to a smooth consistency. Add the oil and blend again.

3 Divide the mixture between 6 small glass dishes, then refrigerate until set.

4 Decorate each serving with a sliced strawberry or some slivers of kiwi fruit. Serve with coconut cream, if liked.

AFFORDABILITY
2

Chewy Cherry BITES

AFFORDABILITY
2

1 Line a 4½ inch square container with plastic wrap.

2 Put the dates and oats into a food processor and process to fine crumbs. Add the blueberries, cranberries, goji berries, chia seeds, and vinegar and process again until the mixture starts to clump together.

3 Turn our the mixture into the prepared container and press down firmly in an even layer using your hands. Let stand for 2-3 hours, until slightly firm. Serve cut into 9 small squares.

4 pitted dates
1 cup jumbo rolled oats
½ cup dried blueberries
½ cup dried cranberries
¼ cup goji berries
¼ cup chia seeds
1 teaspoon apple cider vinegar

Makes **9**
Prep time **10 minutes, plus standing**

COCONUT BALLS

3½ cups shredded fresh coconut or unsweetened dry coconut softened with a little cold water
1½ cups sugar
1¼ cups water
a few drops of food colouring (optional)

Makes **12**
Preparation time **15 minutes,** **plus cooling and setting**
Cooking time **20 minutes**

1 Mix the coconut, sugar, and measured water together. If you want colored balls, divide the mixture between 2, 3, or more dishes (one for each color) and mix a drop or two of food colouring to each, leaving one without coloring if you want white balls. One at a time, stir each mixture in a clean saucepan over low heat until almost all of the syrup has evaporated.

2 One at a time, shape a tablespoonful of the mixture into a ball and place on a baking sheet lined with wax paper. Once all the mixture has been used, you should have 12 balls.

3 Let cool for about 1 hour to harden the outside a little, leaving the insides soft.

VARIATION
For sticky coconut sauce, follow the method as above, adding ⅛ teaspoon of salt and cooking over low heat until a sticky caramel sauce has formed. Do not let it thicken to a point where it will harden. Use this sauce over black glutinous rice or steamed glutinous rice with coconut milk.

AFFORDABILITY 1

ALMOND & WALNUT FUDGE

1 cup almonds
²/₃ cup walnuts
¼ cup coconut oil
1 banana
1 teaspoon vanilla extract
2 tablespoons almond butter
3 tablespoons coconut blossom nectar
2 large pitted dates
good pinch of sea salt

Makes **15**
Prep time **10 minutes, plus soaking and freezing**

AFFORDABILITY
3

1 Put the almonds and walnuts into separate bowls, cover with cold water, and let soak for several hours or overnight.

2 Put the coconut oil into a small heatproof bowl and stand it in a larger heatproof bowl of boiling water. Let melt.

3 Line a small container, about 6 inches square, with plastic wrap.

4 Thoroughly drain the nuts, keeping them separate. Chop the walnuts and set aside.

5 Transfer the almonds to a food processor and process until finely ground. Coarsely chop up the banana and add to the processor along with the melted coconut oil, vanilla extract, almond butter, coconut blossom nectar, dates, and salt. Process to a thick paste. Remove the blade and stir in the walnuts by hand.

6 Turn out the mixture into the prepared container, level the surface, and press down firmly. Freeze for about 1 hour, until firm. Serve cut into small squares.

Watermelon & Lime GRENADINE SQUARES

1   Put the grenadine, sugar, and lime zest and juice along with the measured water into a small saucepan and bring to a boil. Reduce the heat and cook gently for 6–8 minutes, until thick and syrupy. Remove from the heat and let cool.

2   Meanwhile, halve the watermelon and, using a sharp knife, slice the rind from the bottom of each half.

3   Lay the halves on a cutting board and, working from top to bottom, trim the rind from the watermelon flesh in 4 cuts, creating 2 large squares.

4   Cut each square of watermelon into even, bite-size squares and place on a serving platter to form a neat large square (made up of the bite-size squares).

5   Drizzle the cooled grenadine syrup over the top, sprinkle with the lime zest, and serve immediately.

¼ cup grenadine
¼ cup sugar
finely grated zest and juice of
   1 lime, plus extra lime zest to
   decorate
½ cup water
1 small watermelon

Serves **4**
Prep time **20 minutes**

AFFORDABILITY 1

Blueberry & Pear SLUMP

2 large ripe pears, peeled, cored, and chopped
1⅓ cups blueberries
⅓ cup sugar
1⅓ cups all-purpose flour
1 teaspoon baking powder
½ cup almond meal
¼ cup dairy-free spread, diced
⅔ cup almond milk
¼ cup slivered almonds

Serves **4**
Prep time **20 minutes**
Cooking time **25-30 minutes**

AFFORDABILITY **1**

1 Divide the pears and blueberries among 4 large ramekins and sprinkle with 2 tablespoons of the sugar.

2 Sift the flour and baking powder together into a bowl and stir in the almond meal and 2 tablespoons of the remaining sugar. Add the spread and rub in with your fingertips. Stir in the almond milk to make a sticky dough.

3 Dot small spoonfuls of the dough over the fruit and sprinkle with the remaining tablespoon of sugar and the slivered almonds. Bake in a preheated oven, at 375°F, for 25-30 minutes, until the fruit is soft and the topping is golden.

STUDENT TIP

SEPARATE SHELF Chances are you'll need to buy a lot of separate food items (nondairy spreads, cheese, and yogurts, for example), so keep a shelf in the refrigerator and pantry that's dedicated to vegan food. That way, there won't be any mix ups when reaching for a vegan item.

COCONUT
RICE PUDDING

AFFORDABILITY 1

1 Put the rice into a saucepan with the sugar, coconut milk, and measured water.

2 Bring the mixture to a boil, stirring, then pour it into a shallow 1½ quart ovenproof dish. Bake in a preheated oven, at 300°F, for 1 hour 25 minutes, stirring occasionally, until the rice is tender and the liquid is absorbed.

3 Mix the mango and lime zest and juice together in a bowl and serve with the warm or cold rice pudding.

VARIATION

For coconut rice pudding brûlée, bring the rice, sugar, coconut milk, and water to a boil, stirring, as above, then let simmer on the stove, stirring occasionally, for 20 minutes, or according to package directions, until the rice is tender and the liquid is absorbed. Spoon the mixture into individual heatproof ramekins, level the surface, and let cool. Chill for 2–3 hours or overnight. Just before serving, sprinkle 1 tablespoon of demerara sugar or sugar crystals evenly over the surface of each dish. Place under a hot broiler or use a chef's kitchen torch to melt and caramelize the sugar. Let cool for 10 minutes to harden the caramel before serving with chopped mango or rhubarb compote.

⅓ cup jasmine rice or
  short-grain rice
¼ cup sugar
1⅔ cups coconut milk
1⅔ cups water
1 ripe mango, peeled, pitted,
  and chopped
finely grated zest and juice of
  1 lime

Serves **4**
Prep time **15 minutes**
Cooking time **1½ hours**

RAW GINGERBREAD COOKIES

1 cup pecans, plus 15 pecan halves to decorate
2/3 cup raisins
1½ cups rolled oats
¼ cup packed coconut palm sugar or dark brown sugar
1 teaspoon ground ginger
1 teaspoon allspice
¼ teaspoon ground cloves
good pinch of hot chili powder

Makes **15**
Prep time **15 minutes, plus soaking and standing**

1 Put the pecans into a bowl, cover with cold water, and let soak for several hours or overnight. Drain and pat dry with paper towels.

2 Transfer the nuts to a food processor, add the raisins and 1¼ cups of the oats, and process until the mixture forms fine crumbs. Add the palm sugar or brown sugar and spices, then process again until the dough starts to clump together. Add the remaining oats and pulse briefly to combine.

3 Divide the dough into 15 pieces, then shape into balls. Using a 2 inch cookie cutter, cut cookies out of the dough, and press a pecan half into the center of each one. Repeat with the remaining balls. Serve immediately or store in an airtight container for several days.

AFFORDABILITY
2

RAW SALTED PECAN BROWNIES

1 Put the pecans into a bowl, cover with cold water, and let soak for several hours or overnight.

2 Line a 6 inch square shallow baking pan or similar-size container with plastic wrap or parchment paper.

3 Drain the nuts and pat dry with paper towels, then transfer to a food processor and process briefly until chopped. Remove half the nuts and set aside.

4 Continue to process the remaining nuts until finely ground. Add the dates, maple syrup, cacao powder, and salt and process thoroughly, scraping down the mixture from the sides of the bowl, until it forms a thick paste. Add the reserved chopped nuts and pulse briefly until combined. Turn the paste into the prepared pan and press down firmly.

5 To make the topping, wipe out the processor, add the dates and salt, and process to a paste. Add the maple syrup and enough of the measured water to form a spreadable paste.

6 Lift the brownie slab out of the pan and peel away the plastic wrap or paper. Spread over the topping, cut into 16 small squares, and serve.

1½ cups pecans
2¾ cup coarsely chopped pitted dates
¼ cup maple syrup
¾ cup cacao powder
good pinch of salt

Topping
⅔ cup coarsely chopped pitted dates
½ teaspoon sea salt
1 tablespoon maple syrup
3-4 tablespoons water

Makes **16**
Prep time **10 minutes, plus soaking**

AFFORDABILITY
2

ULTRARICH
CHOCOLATE
STACKS

5 oz bittersweet dairy-free
  chocolate, broken into pieces
½ cup coconut cream (not
  sweetened creamed coconut)
1 tablespoon mint leaves
1 cup raspberries
½ teaspoon unsweetened
  cocoa powder
½ teaspoon confectioners' sugar

Serves **4**
Prep time **20 minutes,
  plus chilling**

1 Put the chocolate into a heatproof bowl and set over
  a saucepan of hot water, making sure the bottom of the
  bowl does not touch the water. Stir until melted.

2 Line a baking sheet with parchment paper and spoon
  12 spoonfuls of the melted chocolate onto the sheet.
  Let the chocolate spread into about 3 inch disks, then
  refrigerate for 30 minutes, until set.

3 Whip the coconut cream in a bowl until thick. Place a
  chocolate disk onto a serving plate and spoon some coconut
  cream, mint leaves, and raspberries on top. Place another
  chocolate disk on top and spoon some more coconut cream,
  mint leaves, and raspberries on top. Finish with a third
  chocolate disk. Repeat with the remaining chocolate disks.

4 Mix the cocoa and confectioners' sugar together, then sift
  over the chocolate stacks to serve.

VARIATION
For chocolate & orange stacks, melt the chocolate as above, then
stir in the finely grated zest of 1 orange. Spoon onto a lined baking
sheet and refrigerate until set as above. Whip the coconut cream
as above, then use to layer the disks in stacks of 3 along with
1 well-drained (11 oz) can mandarin orange sections in juice. Dust
with unsweetened cocoa powder to serve.

BANANA FRITTERS
& cinnamon sugar

AFFORDABILITY
1

1. Mix the flour, nutmeg, and 1 teaspoon of the cinnamon together in a bowl, then make a well in the center. Gradually add and beat in enough of the sparkling water to make a smooth batter thick enough to coat the back of a spoon. Let stand for 20 minutes.

2. Fill a deep saucepan one-third full with oil and heat to 350–375°F, or until a cube of bread browns in 30 seconds.

3. Using a pair of tongs, dip the banana pieces, in batches, into the batter, gently lower into the hot oil, and cook for 30 seconds–1 minute, until golden and crisp. Be careful to avoid overcrowding the pan with too many at a time, because they will stick together and the oil temperature will drop.

4. Remove from the pan with a slotted spoon and drain on paper towels.

5. Mix the sugars with the remaining cinnamon, then sprinkle the mixture over the hot fritters to serve.

1¾ cups all-purpose flour
½ teaspoon ground nutmeg
2 teaspoons ground cinnamon
1½ cups sparkling water
sunflower oil, for deep-frying
4 bananas, halved both lengthwise
   and widthwise
3 tablespoons demerara sugar
   or sugar crystals
1 tablespoon granulated sugar

Serves **4**
Prep time **20 minutes,**
   plus standing
Cooking time **5 minutes**

Raw BANANA-CARAMEL PIE

1 Put all the nuts into a bowl, cover with cold water, and let soak for several hours or overnight.

2 Thoroughly drain the nuts, then transfer to a food processor. Add the hemp seeds and process until finely ground. Add 4 of the dates and a pinch of salt and process again until the mixture starts to cling together.

3 Transfer to an 8–8½ inch loose-bottomed tart pan. Using the back of a spoon, press the mixture firmly up the sides and into the bottom of the pan. Chill.

4 Meanwhile, put the remaining dates into a blender with the coconut water, vanilla extract, and a pinch of salt and blend to a thick, smooth paste. Press 2 tablespoons of the paste through a strainer to extract as much pulp as possible, scraping the mixture from the bottom of the strainer, then mix with the maple syrup to make a puree. Set aside the paste and the puree.

5 Toss the bananas with the lemon juice. Arrange two-thirds over the bottom layer and spread with the date paste.

6 Scrape off the top thick layer of coconut cream into a bowl. Reserve 3-4 tablespoons of the liquid from the can, then add the remaining can liquid to the bowl. Beat until thickened and softly peaking, adding some of the reserved liquid if the cream seems too stiff. Beat in the agave syrup, then spread over the filling.

7 Sprinkle with the remaining bananas and drizzle with the reserved date puree. Chill until ready to serve.

½ cup Brazil nuts
¾ cup almonds
¼ cup hemp seeds
2½ cups pitted dates
½ cup coconut water
2 teaspoons vanilla extract
1 tablespoon maple syrup
3 large or 4 medium bananas, sliced
1 tablespoon lemon juice
1 (13½ oz) can coconut cream (not sweetened creamed coconut), chilled overnight
2 tablespoons agave syrup
sea salt

Serves **8**
Prep time **25 minutes, plus overnight chilling and soaking**

RAW STRAWBERRY & VANILLA
CHEESECAKE

1 Put the almonds and cashew nuts into separate bowls, cover with cold water, and let soak for several hours or overnight.

2 Thoroughly drain the almonds, then transfer to a food processor and process until finely chopped. Add the dates and coconut flour and process again until the consistency of finely ground cookies and starting to cling together.

3 Using the back of a spoon, press the mixture firmly into the bottom and slightly up the sides of an 8 inch loose-bottom cake pan. Chill.

4 Meanwhile, put the coconut oil into a small heatproof bowl and stand it in a larger heatproof bowl of boiling water. Let it melt.

5 Thoroughly drain the cashew nuts. Split the vanilla bean open and scrape out the seeds with the tip of a knife. Put the vanilla seeds into a food processor with the cashew nuts and coconut water and process until smooth, scraping down the mixture from the sides of the bowl.

6 Add the melted coconut oil, agave syrup, and lemon juice and process again until pale and smooth.

7 Arrange half the strawberries over the almond layer. Spoon half the cashew filling on top and spread level. Sprinkle with the remaining strawberries, then top with the remaining filling and spread level.

8 Freeze for 3–4 hours, until firm. Loosen the edges of the cheesecake and remove from the pan. Transfer to a serving plate while still semifrozen and let soften in the refrigerator for a couple of hours, or until ready to serve. Serve decorated with extra strawberries.

1 cup almonds
2 cups cashew nuts
6 pitted dates
3 tablespoons coconut flour
1/3 cup coconut oil
1 vanilla bean
1 1/4 cups coconut water
1/3 cup agave syrup
1 tablespoon lemon juice
2 cups hulled and thinly sliced
   strawberries, plus extra to serve

Serves **8-10**
Prep time **25 minutes,**
   plus soaking and chilling

RAW
CHOCOLATE
MUD PIE

1. Put the cashew nuts and hazelnuts into separate bowls, cover with cold water, and let soak for several hours or overnight. Thoroughly drain the nuts, keeping them separate.

2. Transfer 1 cup of the hazelnuts to a food processor and process until chopped. Add 1 cup of the apricots and the cinnamon and process again until the mixture starts to stick together.

3. Transfer to an 8 inch loose-bottom tart pan. Using the back of a spoon, press the mixture firmly up the sides and into the bottom of the pan. Chill.

4. Meanwhile, put the cacao butter in a small heatproof bowl and stand it in a larger heatproof bowl of boiling water. Let melt.

5. Put the cashew nuts, almond milk, vanilla, cacao powder, and agave syrup into a food processor and process until completely smooth, scraping down the mixture from the sides of the bowl. Add the melted cacao butter and process to combine. Turn onto the bottom layer and spread level. Freeze for 30 minutes or chill for 2–3 hours, until firm.

6. Chop the remaining hazelnuts and apricots and sprinkle them over the pie. Blend together the remaining cacao powder and agave syrup in a bowl to make a smooth syrup.

7. Transfer the pie to a plate and drizzle with the syrup to serve.

1½ cups cashew nuts
1 cup plus 2 tablespoons hazelnuts
1⅓ cups dried apricots
1 teaspoon ground cinnamon
¼ cup cacao butter
1 cup almond milk
1 vanilla bean, chopped into small pieces
½ cup cacao powder, plus 1 tablespoon
½ cup agave syrup, plus 3 tablespoons

Serves **8–10**
Prep time **20 minutes, plus chilling and soaking**

AFFORDABILITY
2

CHOCOLATE MOUSSE CAKES
WITH SUMMER BERRIES

1 Cut 6 (6 inch) squares of parchment paper. Press a square over an upturned dariole mold, creasing it down the sides to fit. Lift away and push the paper into the mold to form a lining. (Creasing it over the outside of the mold first makes it easier to fit neatly inside.) Repeat to line another 5 molds. Alternatively, line 6 sections of a cupcake pan with paper cupcake liners.

2 Put the coconut oil into a small heatproof bowl and stand it in a larger heatproof bowl of boiling water. Let melt.

3 Put the avocados, cacao powder, agave syrup, vanilla extract, and lemon juice into a food processor and process until smooth, scraping down the mixture from the sides of the bowl. Add the melted coconut oil and process again. Spoon the mixture into the prepared molds or cupcake liners and chill for several hours or overnight. Top the cakes with the raspberries and blueberries or blackberries and serve.

⅓ cup coconut oil
2 ripe avocados
½ cup cacao powder
½ cup agave syrup
2 teaspoons vanilla extract
squeeze of lemon juice
½ cup raspberries
⅓ cup blueberries or halved
   blackberries

Makes **6**
Prep time **25 minutes,
   plus chilling**

RAW CARROT CAKE
with lime cashew frosting

1 Put the cashew nuts into a bowl, cover with cold water, and let soak for several hours or overnight.

2 Line 2 (6 inch) round cake pans with plastic wrap.

3 Finely shred the carrots and pat dry between several thicknesses of paper towels.

4 Put the pineapple and spices into a food processor and process until chopped. Add the figs and process again until the mixture starts to cling together. Add the carrots, raisins, and oats and process until evenly combined.

5 Divide between the prepared pans and press down firmly. Chill for several hours or freeze for 30 minutes, until firm.

6 To make the frosting, thoroughly drain the nuts, then transfer to a food processor, add the almond milk, and process until smooth. Add the maple syrup along with the lime zest and juice and thoroughly process until thick, spreadable, and smooth, frequently scraping down the mixture from the sides of the bowl.

7 Carefully turn out one of the carrot cakes onto a flat serving plate and peel away the plastic wrap. Spread with half the frosting and top with the second cake. Spread with the remaining frosting and chill until ready to serve. Serve sprinkled with edible flowers, if you want.

8 carrots (about 1 lb)
2/3 cup soft dried pineapple
1 teaspoon ground ginger
¼ teaspoon ground allspice
¾ cup dried figs, stems removed
½ cup golden raisins
2 cups rolled oats
edible flowers, to decorate (optional)

Lime cashew frosting
1 cup cashew nuts
1/3 cup almond milk
¼ cup maple syrup
finely grated zest of 1 lime, plus 3 teaspoons juice

Serves **10**
Prep time **20 minutes, plus chilling and soaking**

RAW CHERRY & ALMOND CAKE
with Chocolate Ganache

1½ cups almonds
¼ cup cacao butter
1 teaspoon almond extract
⅔ cup coconut flour
3 tablespoons packed coconut
   palm sugar or dark brown sugar
2 cups pitted fresh cherries,
   chopped, plus extra to decorate

Ganache
1 cup coconut oil
2 cups cacao powder
1 cup agave syrup

Serves **10**
Prep time **25 minutes,
   plus soaking and chilling**

1 Put the almonds into a bowl, cover with cold water, and let soak for several hours or overnight.

2 Line 2 (6 inch) round cake pans with plastic wrap.

3 To make the ganache, put the coconut oil into a small heatproof bowl and stand it in a larger heatproof bowl of boiling water. Let melt. Pour into a food processor, add the cacao powder and agave syrup, and process until thick and glossy. Transfer to a clean heatproof bowl and set aside.

4 Put the cacao butter into a small heatproof bowl and stand it in a larger heatproof bowl of boiling water. Let melt.

5 Thoroughly drain the nuts, then transfer to the food processor (there's no need to clean it). Add ¼ cup of the chocolate ganache, the almond extract, coconut flour, coconut sugar or dark brown sugar, and melted cacao butter. Process until combined. Remove the blade from the processor and stir in the chopped cherries.

6 Divide the mixture between the prepared pans and press down firmly. Chill for at least 3 hours.

7 Carefully turn out one of the cakes onto a flat serving plate and peel away the plastic wrap. Spread with one-third of the ganache mixture. (If the ganache has solidified, stand the bowl in a larger heatproof bowl of boiling water and let stand until softened, stirring frequently.) Place the second cake on top and spread the top and sides with the remaining ganache. Serve decorated with extra cherries.

BANANA & STRAWBERRY
ice cream

1¾ cups prepared vanilla pudding
  (use a vegan instant pudding
  mix and plant-based milk,
  following package directions)
1 cup soy cream
3 bananas, coarsely chopped
1¼ cups hulled strawberries
3 tablespoons maple syrup

Serves **6**
Prep time **30 minutes, plus
  freezing**

1 Blend the vanilla pudding, cream, bananas, half the strawberries, and the maple syrup together in a blender or food processor until smooth.

2 Pour the mixture into a freezerproof container and freeze for 3 hours, until just starting to freeze around the edges.

3 Scrape the mixture into a bowl and beat with a handheld blender or spatula until smooth.

4 Finely chop the remaining strawberries, stir into the mixture, and return to the container. Freeze for 3-4 hours or overnight until firm. Let soften for 15 minutes before serving.

AFFORDABILITY
1

STUDENT TIP

FAT CAN BE FRIENDLY This is especially true for vegans. Don't be fooled by low-fat versions of nondairy milk, yogurt, and cheese. The fat is often replaced by low-nutritious alternatives and your body needs a certain amount of fats for energy.

Raspberry, Pistachio & Rose
SEMIFREDDO

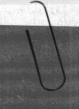

1 Put the pistachios into a bowl, cover with cold water, and let soak for several hours or overnight.

2 Line a small 2½ cup loaf pan or similar-size freezerproof container with plastic wrap.

3 Coarsely mash the raspberries with a fork. Drain the nuts, then coarsely chop.

4 Scrape off the top thick layer of coconut cream into a bowl. Set aside 3-4 tablespoons of the liquid from the can, then add the remaining liquid to the bowl. Beat with a spoon until thickened and softly peaking, adding some of the reserved liquid if the cream seems too stiff. Beat in the agave syrup and rose extract.

5 Gently stir in the pistachios and raspberries and transfer the mixture to the prepared pan. Spread the surface level and freeze for at least 4 hours or overnight, until firm.

6 If frozen overnight, transfer the semifreddo to the refrigerator about 1 hour before serving. Invert onto a plate or board and peel away the plastic wrap. Cut into slices and serve sprinkled with extra raspberries.

⅔ cup shelled pistachios
1 cup raspberries, plus extra
  to serve
1 (13½ oz) can coconut cream,
  chilled overnight
3 tablespoons agave syrup
1 teaspoon rose extract

Makes **6**
Prep time **10 minutes, plus
  overnight soaking, chilling,
  and freezing**

AFFORDABILITY 1

Watermelon
SORBET

10 cups seeded watermelon cubes
juice of 1 orange
zest of ½ orange
½ inch piece of fresh ginger root,
  peeled and thinly sliced

Serves **4-6**
Prep time **10 minutes,**
  plus freezing

1 Put the watermelon cubes, orange juice, orange zest, and ginger into a food processor or blender. Process for 1-2 minutes, until smooth.

2 Pour the mixture into a freezerproof container and freeze for 1½ hours, or until halfway frozen. Remove the mixture from the freezer and whisk. Return to the container. Whisk at least twice again during the freezing time. There should be plenty of air whipped into the sorbet or it will be too icy and hard. Cover and freeze completely.

VARIATION
For cantaloupe & lychee sorbet, replace the watermelon with 1 ripe medium cantaloupe, peeled, seeded, and cut into 1 inch pieces. Replace the orange juice and zest with juice and zest from ½ a lime. Process the cantaloupe in a mixer for 2-3 minutes, or until smooth. Add the flesh from 1 (20 oz) can of lychees (reserve the syrup) and give a few more pulses, then pour the mixture into a bowl. Warm the lychee syrup with a ½ inch piece of fresh ginger root, finely grated, for 2-3 minutes. Let cool before adding it to the cantaloupe and lychee mixture. Whisk twice during freezing.

AFFORDABILITY

1

APPLE, PEACH & STRAWBERRY ICE POPS

1 Halve the peaches, remove the pits, coarsely chop the flesh, and juice in a blender or food processor.

2 Add one-third of the water and spoon the mixture into 3-4 ice pop molds. Freeze until just set.

3 Coarsely chop the apple, then juice in a blender or food processor. Add one-third of the water and pour over the frozen peach mixture. Freeze until just set.

4 Hull the strawberries, then juice them in a blender or food processor. Add the remainder of the water, pour over the frozen apple mixture, and freeze until set.

VARIATION
For orange & strawberry juice, hull 1⅓ cups strawberries and juice them with 2 oranges.

2 peaches
1¼ cups water
1 red apple
1 cup strawberries

Makes **3-4**
Prep time **10 minutes,
    plus freezing**

AFFORDABILITY
1

BACK TO BASICS

SALAD DRESSING

CREPES

VEGETABLE BROTH

CREPES

2 cups whole-wheat flour
2 teaspoons baking powder
pinch of salt
2 cups rice milk or soy milk
1 tablespoon lime juice
canola oil, for frying

Serves **4**
Prep time **5 minutes**
Cooking time **10 minutes**

1 Mix the flour, baking powder, and salt with the milk and lime juice and beat together to make a smooth batter.

2 Heat a heavy nonstick skillet until hot, then pour in a dribble of canola oil and swirl it around the pan.

3 Add just enough batter to barely cover the bottom of the pan in a thin, even layer. Cook for about a minute, until the bottom has set and become lightly browned, then flip the crepe over and cook the other side.

4 Serve the crepes hot, spread with vegan cream cheese and preserves or maple syrup. If you prefer a savory breakfast, top the crepes with the cream cheese plus yeast extract and pickles.

AFFORDABILITY 1

Salad DRESSING

¼ cup pumpkin seed oil
  or hempseed oil
1 tablespoon flaxseed oil
2 teaspoons vegan Dijon mustard
1 tablespoon balsamic vinegar
salt and pepper

Serves **4**
Prep time **5 minutes**

1 Mix all the ingredients together and use as required. The dressing will keep for 1 week in the refrigerator.

SOYNNAISE

1 Put the soy milk and salt into a saucepan and heat until hot but not boiling.

2 While whisking the milk with a handheld blender, add the oil and vinegar.

3 Still whisking, add the crushed garlic, if using, mustard, and flaxseed oil. Refrigerate and use as required. It will keep for up to 1 week.

½ cup soy milk
pinch of salt
½ cup sunflower oil
2 teaspoons vegan white wine vinegar
1 garlic clove, crushed (optional)
1 tablespoon vegan Dijon mustard
2 tablespoons flaxseed oil

Serves **4**
Prep time **5-10 minutes**
Cooking time **2 minutes**

VEGETABLE
Broth

1   Put all the ingredients into a large saucepan. Bring to a boil and simmer gently for 30 minutes, skimming when necessary.

2   Strain the broth, cool, then refrigerate it. It will keep for up to a week in the refrigerator, or up to 3 months in the freezer.

3½–4 cups mixed vegetables
   (about 1 lb), excluding potatoes,
   parsnips, or other starchy root
   vegetables, chopped
1 garlic clove
6 peppercorns
1 bouquet garni
5 cups water

Makes **4¼ cups**
Prep time **5–10 minutes**
Cooking time **35 minutes**

AFFORDABILITY
1

INDEX

Acknowledgments

Dreamstime.com Ahidden 23 above left; Alexey Stiop 55 above left; Andrey Maslakov 86; Baibaz 87 below; Brad Calkins 123 right; Cleardesign 54; Dpimborough 123 left; Jabiru 55 below; Lightfieldstudiosprod 22; Lisa870 122; Makik 87 above left; Martinmark 23 below right; Monkey Business Images 138; Mustipan 55 above right; Raluca Tudor 139 above; Richard Griffin 87 above right; Svetlana Kolpakova 139 below; Tommaso79 23 above right; Vadymvdrobot 160.

iStock Geber86 161 above; GMVozd 216; redhumv 214; SolisImages 161 below; sunara 219; sykkel 217.

Octopus Publishing Group Clive Bozzard-Hill 45, 47, 66, 99, 100, 121, 134, 151, 178, 180; Eleanor Skan 119, 127, 212; Gus Filgate 88; Ian Wallace 64; Lis Parsons 10, 11, 13, 15, 48, 53, 59, 68, 133, 187, 192, 194, 198, 199, 203, 204, 205, 206, 207, 209, 211, 213; Neil Mersh 52; Sandra Lane 193; Stephen Conroy 39, 82, 106, 128; Will Heap 34, 51, 56, 57, 61, 65, 73, 79, 80, 81, 85, 112, 125, 129, 131, 140, 189, 190, 195; William Reavell 37; William Shaw 14, 17, 19, 21, 25, 26, 27, 28, 33, 36, 38, 40, 41, 43, 49, 50, 60, 62, 63, 67, 69, 70, 71, 83, 84, 89, 91, 92, 93, 101, 102, 104, 107, 109, 111, 115, 117, 118, 137, 142, 147, 149, 153, 157, 162, 169, 170, 171, 173, 174, 175, 177, 179, 183, 188, 196, 197, 201, 202.

Publisher Sarah Ford
Extra recipes by Joanna Farrow
Features writer Cara Frost-Sharratt
Junior Editor Ella Parsons
Copy Editor Francesca Ryan
Senior Designer Jaz Bahra
Designer Jeremy Tilston
Picture Researcher Jennifer Veall
Production Controller Meskerem
   Berhane